Corie Kline

mural magic

Painting Scenes on Furniture and Walls

 NORTH LIGHT BOOKS, CINCINNATI, OHIO
www.artistsnetwork.com

Other fine North Light Books are available from your local bookstore, art supply store or direct from the publisher. Visit our web site at www.fwmedia.com.

13 12 11 10 09   5 4 3 2 1

Distributed in Canada by Fraser Direct
100 Armstrong Avenue
Georgetown, ON, Canada L7G 5S4
Tel: (905) 877-4411

Distributed in the U.K. and Europe by David & Charles
Brunel House, Newton Abbot, Devon, TQ12 4PU, England
Tel: (+44) 1626 323200, Fax: (+44) 1626 323319
Email: postmaster@davidandcharles.co.uk

Distributed in Australia by Capricorn Link
P.O. Box 704, S. Windsor NSW, 2756 Australia
Tel: (02) 4577-3555

Library of Congress Cataloging in Publication Data
Kline, Corie
  Mural magic : painting scenes on furniture and walls / by Corie
Kline. -- 1st ed.
      p. cm.
  Includes index.
  ISBN 978-1-60061-166-7 (pbk. : alk. paper)
  1. Furniture painting. 2. Mural painting and decoration. 3. Decoration and ornament. I. Title.
  TT199.4.K575 2009
  745.7'23--dc22
                          2008039634

Edited by Jacqueline Musser
Designed by Clare Finney
Production coordinated by Matt Wagner
Photographed by Christine Polomsky and Ric Deliantoni

ABOUT THE AUTHOR

Corie Kline is a professional artist who runs her own painted furniture and mural business called "You're Art!". She received her BFA with Teaching Certification from Bowling Green State University and then officially began her artistic career as an art teacher. After starting a family, she became a stay-at-home mom and began to paint for clients on their walls and furniture.

Corie exhibits and sells her painted furniture at art shows and has painted murals in private homes, businesses and schools. You may view her portfolio at www.youreart.com.

Corie lives in Cincinnati, Ohio, with her husband, Jared, her twin daughters, Celia and Mallory, and her youngest daughter, Marin.

METRIC CONVERSION CHART

To convert	to	multiply by
Inches	Centimeters	2.54
Centimeters	Inches	0.4
Feet	Centimeters	30.5
Centimeters	Feet	0.03
Yards	Meters	0.9
Meters	Yards	1.1

ACKNOWLEDGMENTS

I must first thank the talented folks at F+W Media, Inc., who approached me for this book right when I thought it would be fun to write one. I will never know all the work that goes on behind the scenes, but my gratitude is endless. Special thanks to my editor, Jacqueline Musser, for leading me through this daunting process, making it seem easy along the way.

Thank you to the Bernicke, Brisben, Jansen, Nachtrab, and Slee families for letting me borrow your walls to make this book come to life.

Special thanks to my girls, Celia, Mallory and Marin, for being such great kids and for understanding that even though I am a stay-at-home mom, I still run out to go "paint at a lady's house." You simply fulfill my life.

Thank you to my awesome friends and family who have opened their homes to my children so that I may paint. Your willingness to help at a moment's notice has facilitated my career and enabled me to take it to the next level.

I reserve my deepest gratitude for my husband, Jared, for his love and support and for always pushing me to be a better artist. He has spent countless hours assembling, repairing and carrying furniture all over creation, in addition to keeping me on my toes with how to run a business. I could not do this without you.

And a final thank you goes to all the people who have offered me their business or kind words as a result of my art. You make being creative a way of life!

DEDICATION

This book is first dedicated to my mom, for giving me my first "how-to" craft book at age nine and saying, "Here, see if you can make these." Her artistic talents rubbed off on me, and my love of art stems from her constantly being thrilled and impressed at whatever I create. And secondly to my dad, for giving me patience, precision and the eye for detail. Thank you for being such wonderful parents and creative people!

contents

introduction

As a person who likes to combine art with function, I have always been drawn to painting furniture. Whether the piece is old or new, I love treating it like a blank canvas and working a design around corners and over drawers. I don't let its shape limit me and by doing this, I'm able to transform the furniture into a mini mural. It becomes a truly functional work of art.

Wall murals are a great way to create a whole new setting in a room. They can give a different feel to a space every time you enter it. They are planned out in size and design to truly customize the room and meet the specific needs of the owner. Although they can easily be painted over, wall murals are usually treated as artwork that will remain in the space for a while. Because of this, they often require a strong commitment to the theme and coordinating décor.

What if we combine the functionality of painted furniture with the atmosphere of a wall mural? We get Mural Magic!

Combining the look of hand-painted furniture with its very own matching wall mural will give you an artistic setting that will transform any space or room. My hope with this book is to inspire you to create a special setting of your own. We all have a piece of furniture that needs updating. Why not update the little nook that it lives in as well? My painting style will show you how to render objects realistically and include details in a scene with minimal effort. I will provide you with step-by-step instructions on how to create each project, using very few materials outside of paint, a few brushes and some water.

Painting the wall space around your hand-painted furniture will give your décor the ultimate wow factor. Grab your paint brushes and start creating your own mural magic!

materials

PREPPING AND FINISHING SUPPLIES

These tools will be helpful in preparing your surfaces for paint, as well as protecting your decorative painting in the end (see page 11 for a photo of these materials):

- Handheld electric sander
- Sandpaper
- Wood filler
- Putty knife
- Paper towels
- KILZ 2 Interior/Exterior Primer
- Polycrylic Protective Finish (Clear Satin) by Minwax

PAINT

For all my decorative painting and wall murals, I use acrylic paint sold in small squeeze bottles. They are easy to use, and I love that they come in just about any color imaginable. The paint is very rich in color, despite being very inexpensive, and can easily be cleaned up with soap and water. I use three different brands depending on what color I need: Delta Ceramcoat acrylics, Apple Barrel acrylics, and DecoArt Americana acrylics. All are easy to blend and work very well together.

If I need a neutral color in a larger quantity, I use Painter's Touch or American Accents by Rust-Oleum. These paints are sold in quart cans and come in a variety of colors that will get you started for quite a few projects, especially if the surface requires several coats of paint.

BRUSHES

For a lot of my basecoating and finishing, I use simple, inexpensive chip brushes. They are flexible, soft and are practically disposable. Their only drawback is that they shed easily when they are new, so break them in by running them along your hand and pulling at the bristles a bit.

Here is a visual reference for each of the paint colors used in the book. Each project includes a list of the paints used for easy reference.

APPLE BARREL ACRYLICS

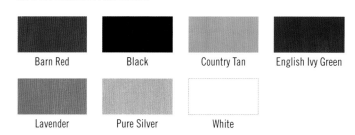

Barn Red — Black — Country Tan — English Ivy Green

Lavender — Pure Silver — White

DECOART AMERICANA ACRYLICS

Canyon Orange — Celery Green — Cocoa — Deep Midnight Blue — Desert Sand

French Grey Blue — French Mauve — Winter Blue — Yellow Ochre

DELTA CERAMCOAT ACRYLICS

Antique White — Blissful Blue — Burnt Sienna — Burnt Umber — Butter Cream

Metallic Gold — Medium Flesh — Midnight Blue — Moss Green — Mudstone

Old Parchment — Royal Plum — Straw — Timberline Green

All my painting projects are completed with just a handful of brushes. I've tried to use others that are fancy shaped and have specific cuts, but I always go back to my favorite flats and rounds. All you need is a few sizes of flats: ½-inch (13mm), ¾-inch (19mm) and 1-inch (25mm), as well as a no. 10 flat. The rounds I use are nos. 4 and 8. A no. 0 liner is also needed for details and fine linework, like in vines or lettering. The bristles are synthetic and keep their shape with proper maintenance (don't let them soak in water for long periods of time; wash them with soap and water after use).

You are only as good as your brush, so invest in decent quality and replace them as soon as the bristles no longer flow the paint onto the surface as they should. Keep a couple of your old flat brushes around, though, as they can be used as scruffy brushes needed to apply texture or foliage.

GENERAL MATERIALS

I try to keep the painting process very simple without using a lot of fancy products or decorative tools to create my projects. All the following supplies can be purchased at home improvement or craft stores, and some you may already have on hand.

Paper or foam plates: I use these as paint palettes. They are lightweight, inexpensive and disposable.

Paper towels: I use sturdy paper towels for blotting out wet brushes, wiping out paint and for general cleanup.

Brush basin: A plastic water basin is nice to have for cleaning your brushes while painting. The one I use has ribs on the bottom to swish brushes against, which gets the paint out of the bristles. It also has two separate water compartments.

Plastic tray: While I paint, I keep my palette plates, paper towels and brush basin together on an old plastic tray to create a transportable working station that can be moved around a room for murals, on and off ladders and kept together on the floor when painting furniture.

SKETCHING TOOLS

There are a few tools needed when sketching or transferring a design onto a wall or piece of furniture.

Water-soluble graphite pencil: Most of my sketching is freehand, and I use a Prismacolor Water Soluble Graphite pencil. The advantage of this type of pencil is that it will easily wipe off of surfaces with a damp paper towel, no erasing needed. I use a white version of the pencil when the surface is painted dark, so the lines will show up. They are sold in most art supply stores.

Carbon paper: If I am transferring lettering or a pattern onto the surface, I use a sheet of carbon paper behind the

These materials will help you paint the projects in this book: 1. Acrylic paints, 2. Spray primer, 3. Chip brush, 4. Latex house paint, 5. Cloud Sponge by Plaid, 6. Natural sea sponges, 7. Carbon paper, 8. Stencil brush, 9. Water-soluble graphite pencil, 10. Artist's brushes.

pattern. Tape it up with low-tack blue painter's tape and trace over the design with a regular pencil. I also keep a Mr. Clean Magic Eraser handy to remove some of the more stubborn pencil or carbon lines. Do not scrub too harshly, as the paint will be removed as well.

Four-foot (1.2m) level: A four-foot (1.2m) level is a great tool when making sure horizon lines are straight, fence posts aren't crooked and faux windows are level. A smaller handheld level is nice, too, for similar situations on furniture. I use these tools frequently and sometimes couple them with a metal yardstick when a measurement is required.

ALTERNATE PAINTING TOOLS

Certain painting techniques call for ways to apply the paint other than with a regular brush. The following items can give you textures a typical brush can't, and they make the process easier.

Stencil brush: I use a stencil brush for spattering paint. Loading the brush with paint and then flicking the stiff bristles will create tiny droplets that resemble sand or grit.

Natural sea sponge: Sea sponges will give you the blurred softness needed to paint clouds or foliage.

4-inch (10cm) foam roller: Foam rollers are excellent for basecoating furniture because they make it easy to apply the paint and they won't leave behind brushstrokes.

Cloud Sponge: One of my favorite products I have discovered is the Cloud Sponge by Plaid. I think its original purpose is to blot on clouds when painting because of its fuzzy surface and formed ridges. I, however, use it to apply paint more accurately when a straight line is needed. A horizon line or tree trunk will look crisp and less wavy when the paint is applied with the edge of a Cloud Sponge, as opposed to a brush where the bristles could wave out when pressure is accidentally varied. One side of the Cloud Sponge is soft and velvety, while the other has a firm texture for gripping. I load the paint on the velvety side of the sponge. I also use the Cloud Sponge for wiping on large areas of paint. The sponge holds a lot of paint, thus making the application much quicker.

surface preparation

Preparing your furniture for painting is one of the most important steps. I'll be honest; I don't know how many times I have wanted to just jump into the fun of decorative painting on a really cool piece, but I knew I had about four steps before I got there. Properly sanding and priming the piece will pay off in the end and make the furniture durable, giving you the results you want.

FILLING IN FLAWS

The first thing I do, whether I am working with a new or old piece, is remove the hardware or drawer pulls. Next, I inspect the piece for deep nicks, gouges or other surface flaws that need to be covered with wood filler. Wood filler is an essential tool in furniture repair and can be found at home improvement stores. I apply it with a putty knife and let it dry overnight before sanding the surface smooth. If the piece is old, not all the imperfections need to be filled, just the ones that may be distracting to the painted design. If the piece is new, sometimes it will have a deep knot or scratch from shipping that I want to hide. I also use wood filler when changing the hardware on a piece of furniture. If I choose to replace the drawer pulls with ones that won't fit in the existing holes, I fill the old holes with wood filler as well. I usually drill the holes for the new hardware once the decorative painting is complete and the piece has its final coat of finish.

I also want to mention here that the new hardware I choose does not always have the right finish or "look" to it when I purchase it. I often use spray paint to change the finish and make it more suitable to the painted piece. Just make sure you spray prime the hardware first before applying the finishing color. I use Painter's Touch Primer and Spray Paint by Rust-Oleum.

SANDING THE SURFACE

After you fill in the flaws, the next step is to sand the surface. I try to sand outdoors or at least away from my work area where I will be painting. This keeps the dust separate so it doesn't end up in the paint. If the piece is old and already has a finish on it, sanding will rough it up and make it suitable to accept the primer. If the piece is new and unfinished, a very light sanding is all you need.

I use a handheld electric sander on as many surfaces as possible, sanding in the direction of the wood grain. Any long plane on a dresser or end table will sand quickly, and some of the nicks will even be softened. Sanding will also smooth out your dried wood filler and blend it into the surface. Use a light grit whenever possible so the sander isn't leaving scratches behind that are hard to cover with the paint. For smaller, tighter areas on the piece or on areas that are rounded, like table legs, I use regular sandpaper and sand by hand.

Once sanding is complete, I remove the dust with damp paper towels. I use a heavy-duty brand, like Bounty, that won't shred when I wipe with it. You can also use a handheld vacuum or old paintbrush to remove dust from hard-to-reach areas.

CHOOSING FURNITURE

WHEN I FIRST STARTED TO PAINT FURNITURE, I shopped at yard sales for cheap yet sturdy pieces with large painting surfaces. My main motivation was for the piece to be both functional and a work of art, so it had to be in decent working order and also still serve a household purpose. I began with small end tables and mini dressers that had great lines to them and required very little repair and no stripping. Because I was selling the furniture I painted, I eventually began to invest in new, unfinished pieces to keep producing some crowd favorites: For example, I had to buy new children's rocking chairs once my used ones sold.

You can find just about any piece of furniture unfinished; however, it can be very pricey and not always constructed as well as an older piece. Sometimes you even have to assemble the new furniture yourself. You have to decide between buying a piece that is old and may require repair and extra surface preparation or buying a more expensive new piece that is readily available.

I have painted both new and old pieces for the projects in this book, and they all have their own charm. My main advice is always keep your eyes open for that cute piece (new or used) and to have your friends start looking, too. I don't know how many phone calls I have received from someone who spotted a piece while shopping or was looking to give away a solid wooden toy box or bedroom dresser. Jump on those opportunities!

PRIMING

Whether the furniture is old or new, it must be primed before you begin the basecoat and decorative painting. Priming serves as a barrier on the existing surface, whether you are blocking out old finish or stains on a used piece or knots and raw wood on a new, unfinished piece. If you don't prime, the old finish or knots will show through your basecoat and decorative finish.

Applying primer will also make the basecoat flow on easier.

I use KILZ 2, a quick-drying, water-based primer that is easy to clean up with soap and water. You can apply the primer with a 2-inch (51mm) chip brush or a 4-inch (10cm) foam roller for larger surfaces.

After the primer has dried, the piece may need another light sanding. I usually find this is the case for the new, unfinished pieces because the primer brings out the wood grain. At this stage, I usually sand lightly by hand.

BASECOAT

Now you are ready for your basecoat. There are two types of basecoat paint I use, depending on the color I need. If I need a neutral background color like white or cream, I use Painter's Touch or American Accents brand paints. Both are latex paints made by Rust-Oleum. They are sold in quarts at home improvement stores and come in a collection of shades. Because I use neutral colors more frequently, I buy them in these larger quantities and always have them on hand. If I need a more specific or brighter color, I use the acrylic craft paint sold in small squeeze bottles at most craft supply stores. The basecoat can be applied with a 2-inch (51mm) chip brush or 4-inch (10cm) foam roller, and you can

These tools are helpful when preparing and finishing your surfaces: 1. KILZ 2 interior/exterior primer, 2. Paper towel, 3. Polycrylic protective finish, 4. Handheld electric sander, 5. Sandpaper, 6. Putty knife, 7. Wood filler.

keep the foam roller moist by wrapping it in a plastic bag between coats.

PROTECTIVE FINISHES

Once all the decorative painting is complete, you must apply a protective finish to preserve your design and make the painted surface durable. I recommend Minwax Polycrylic Protective Finish in Clear Satin or any other water-based polyurethane that is resistant to yellowing over time. I recommend applying three coats of finish using a 2-inch (51mm) chip brush.

There are two things to note when applying the coats of finish. First, watch for drips and runs. When applying the clear finish in certain nooks or corners on the piece of furniture, it is hard to see where too much has collected. There have been times when I have walked away and returned for the

second coat, only to see a run that has dripped down and dried that way. You can fix this by sanding out the run and touching up with the necessary paint color.

The second tip when applying the finish coats is to watch for fuzz or small hairs that land in your wet finish. They aren't noticeable on all basecoat colors, but if one does stick out, you can easily remove it with your fingertip while the finish is still wet; then brush the area smooth again. If the fuzz has dried on the surface (which shows up especially well on a white piece of furniture), try to loosen it with a damp paper towel, rubbing in a small circular motion with your fingernail. Bottom line: It's best not to apply the finish while wearing a fuzzy sweater!

techniques

LOADING A NO. 0 LINER

No. 0 liners are great for detail work and lettering. You have to use thinned paint with this brush so the paint will flow from the brush and make continuous strokes.

1. THIN PAINT TO LOAD IT

Dip the no. 0 liner in water and don't blot it or tap out any water. Place the wet brush over your palette and let the water drop from the brush into the pool of paint you want to load on the brush. Use a circular motion to mix the paint and water so the paint becomes thin. Use the liner to pull out a line of paint onto your palette. Roll your brush as you pull out the paint to create a point on the brush.

2. TEST BRUSH

If the brush is properly loaded, the paint will flow off easily, and you'll be able to make smooth lines ideal for lettering and small details.

Because the brush is so small, expect to reload it frequently.

DOUBLE LOADING

Whenever I need to mix colors, I double load them on my brush and let the colors mix on the surface. Double loading is especially useful for painting flower petals.

1. LOAD FIRST COLOR

Dip your brush in your first color.

2. LOAD SECOND COLOR

Immediately dip your brush in the second color.

3. LET COLORS BLEND

The two colors together will create a blended, variegated color.

4. NOTE COLOR VARIATION

Each stroke you take will produce slightly different shades depending on how the paint was loaded on the brush and how the paint comes off the brush.

FLOATING A CAST SHADOW

Cast shadows help anchor objects in a mural and add depth and realism to the scene.

1. THIN PAINT

Dip a brush in water and don't blot it or shake out the excess water. (I generally use a no. 8 round for my shadows.) Move the brush over your palette and let the water drop from your brush into your shadow color, usually black. Use a circular motion to mix the paint and water and pull the paint out away from the puddle so the paint is thinner.

2. WIPE BRUSH

Wipe your brush on a clean paper towel.

3. LOAD BRUSH

Reload the brush into the inky, thin paint on the palette. The bristles will absorb this thin paint because the brush is drier and not heavy with pigment.

4. SHADE OBJECT

Run the properly loaded brush up against the object that needs to be shaded.

CREATING FOLIAGE WITH A SCRUFFY BRUSH

Old, scruffy brushes are perfect for areas that need a lot of texture but don't need a lot of detail, such as tree foliage.

1. LOAD BRUSH

Load a dry brush with two or three colors. Stamp the colors out on the palette to work them into the brush.

2. POUNCE ON COLOR

Pounce the color onto the surface, letting the brush soften the color as it goes on the surface.

SPATTERING

Spattering is a quick and easy way to add texture to a surface. It works especially well on sand and rocks.

1. LOAD STENCIL BRUSH
Dip a coarse stencil brush in water and blot it dry on a paper towel. Dip the brush into the paint.

2. WORK PAINT INTO BRISTLES
Run your finger over the brush a few times while the brush is over the palette or a paper towel to work the paint into the bristles.

3. FLICK PAINT ONTO SURFACE
Hold your brush over the surface and run your finger over the brush to flick, or spatter, the paint onto the surface.

PAINTING WITH A SYNTHETIC SPONGE

Large, synthetic faux finishing sponges such as a Cloud Sponge by Plaid are great for painting large surfaces quickly and for painting large, straight lines. The bristles of brushes can flare out and make the edges of your straight lines wiggle if you vary your pressure even slightly. Synthetic sponges will give you a straight edge no matter how much you change the pressure.

1. LOAD SPONGE WITH PAINT
Slightly dampen the sponge with clean water and then dip the sponge in paint.

2. APPLY PAINT TO SURFACE
Use even pressure to make a long, straight line with the paint.

PAINTING CLOUDS WITH A SEA SPONGE

You can create light, fluffy clouds with a sea sponge.

1. DAMPEN AND DRY SPONGE
Dip your sponge in water. Wring it out well and then wrap the sponge in a paper towel. Wring out the sponge a second time.

2. DIP SPONGE IN PAINT
Dip one of the edges in a pool of White paint and then pull the paint out onto the palette.

3. WORK PAINT INTO SPONGE
Pounce the sponge on the palette a bit to work the paint into the sponge.

4. APPLY RIDGE OF PAINT
Tap the sponge on the surface, making a ridge of White at the top of the cloud.

5. TURN SPONGE
Turn the sponge to a clean edge.

6. SOFTEN RIDGE OF PAINT
Pounce the clean edge against the ridge of White to soften the cloud. Move down to spread the color out and soften the edges. If your sponge gets too dry, dip it in water again to help soften the paint more.

When I saw this jewelry armoire, I knew it must live out the remainder of its life as a lighthouse! The tapering shape and the flat sides are ideal for painting across with a mural, and the curves at the bottom give it just the right amount of character. The lighthouse design itself is basic, but I will show you how to give it dimension with proper shading and highlights. I basecoated the armoire the same blue as the wall color to tie the two murals together.

The lighthouse serves as a focal point to the wall mural behind it—boats on the horizon. You will learn how to paint the look of water and work with sponges that give you both crisp lines and the soft look of clouds. Put the two murals together, and you have an ocean or lake view right in your home.

by the
sea

materials

For the sailboat mural

BRUSHES
½-inch (13mm) and 1-inch (25mm) flats, No. 10 flat, No. 0 liner, No. 8 round

PALETTE
Apple Barrel Acrylics: Barn Red, Black, Country Tan, English Ivy Green, White

DecoArt Americana Acrylics: Celery Green, Deep Midnight Blue, Winter Blue

Delta Ceramcoat Acrylics: Burnt Umber, Old Parchment

OTHER MATERIALS
4-foot (1.2m) level, Cloud Sponge by Plaid, Natural sea sponge

For the lighthouse jewelry armoire

BRUSHES
½-inch (13mm), ¾-inch (19mm) and 1-inch (25mm) flats, No. 10 flat, No. 0 liner, Nos. 4 and 8 rounds, Stencil brush

PALETTE
Apple Barrel Acrylics: Barn Red, Black, Country Tan, English Ivy Green, White

DecoArt Americana Acrylics: Deep Midnight Blue

Delta Ceramcoat Acrylics: Burnt Umber, Old Parchment

OTHER MATERIALS
Natural sea sponge

PAINTING THE SAILBOAT MURAL

As you start to sketch the mural, use a 4-foot (1.2m) level to mark off your horizon line. The wall color is latex house paint, Martha Stewart One Coat Bluepoint.

1 BLOCK IN DESIGN

Use the Cloud Sponge to basecoat the water with Deep Midnight Blue. Switch to the 1-inch (25mm) flat to add and blend in Winter Blue for some of the lighter areas. Also add a wash of Celery Green in just a few places. Paint in the entire water area. The boats will go on top of the water.

Use a 1-inch (25mm) flat to place the distant beach with Country Tan. Add Burnt Umber for the darks. This coastline doesn't need to be straight and smooth. Bumps and wiggles will appear as mounds in the sand.

Use a damp sea sponge to place the shrubs. Start by stamping on the dark foliage with a mix of English Ivy Green and Black. Then place highlights with Old Parchment.

Double load a ½-inch (13mm) flat with Country Tan and Burnt Umber and paint the boats. Make the boats slightly curved at the top and straighter at the bottom so it looks like they are sitting in the water.

Basecoat the sails with two coats of White and the ½-inch (13mm) brush.

2 DETAIL SAILS

Shade the left sides of the sails with a ½-inch (13mm) flat double loaded with Black and White to make a gray. Use the chisel edge of the brush to create a line of gray that defines the bottom of the sails. Also shade the white cabins on the tops of the decks.

3 BASECOAT RED DETAILS

Basecoat the red flags with Barn Red and the ½-inch (13mm) flat. Basecoat the middle boat with Barn Red. Add a red line to the inside of the boat on the left.

4 SHADE, HIGHLIGHT RED DETAILS

Shade the red areas with a no. 10 flat double loaded with Barn Red and Black. Place a dark shadow on the bottom of each flag and on the bottom of the red boat. Then blend in a highlight by double loading the no. 10 flat with Barn Red and White. The highlight is on the tops of the red areas.

5 ADD STRIPES TO SAILS

Use the no. 10 flat to add stripes to the sails. The stripes are Old Parchment, Barn Red and Deep Midnight Blue. Make the stripes curved. Start at the outside of the sail and move inward toward the mast. Use the flat of the brush for the larger stripes and the chisel edge of the brush for the smaller stripes. Also add stripes to the boats.

6 PAINT MASTS, ADD SHADING

Add the masts and booms with Country Tan and the chisel edge of the no. 10 flat. Occasionally pick up some Burnt Umber with the Country Tan for shaded areas.

Switch to a no. 8 round and float some thin Black beneath the sails and down along the inside of the boats for additional shading (see page 13).

Outline the windows on the cabins with the no. 0 liner double loaded with Black and a bit of White.

tip Adding stripes to the sails is a great way to tie in accent colors in your mural. Use any color combination that works with your room décor. Also, feel free to personalize your boats with names and numbers to symbolize important dates.

7 ADD RIPPLES TO WATER

Double load the no. 8 round with Deep Midnight Blue and a bit of Winter Blue and float some ripples and waves over the bottoms of the boats. The waves will extend slightly behind the boats to show their wakes. You can also place additional ripple lines throughout the water.

THE FINISHED MURAL

PAINTING THE LIGHTHOUSE JEWELRY ARMOIRE

Basecoat the entire piece with two coats of a light blue latex house paint that matches your wall color. For this project, I used a latex paint, Martha Stewart One Coat Bluepoint.

Sketch out the design of the lighthouse. The design is basically the same on each side of the piece, but the windows and doors are placed in slightly different locations on each side. You'll complete each step three times (once on each side of the dresser) before moving on to the next step.

1 BLOCK IN LIGHTHOUSE

Basecoat the lighthouse with White and the 1-inch (25mm) flat. Because the drawers on this piece of furniture are flush, I simply painted over all divisions, treating the surface as one solid piece. For the top, the blue areas are Deep Midnight Blue, and the red areas are Barn Red. Use a 1-inch (25mm) flat for large areas and a no. 10 flat for smaller areas.

2 SHADE WHITE BASE

Load the 1-inch (25mm) flat with White and pick up a little thinned Black to shade the white base of the lighthouse. The Black should blend with the White on the brush to create a soft gray. The shading is darker on the sides and lighter in the center to show the roundness of the building. Also, be sure to shade darker under the dark blue collar.

3 PAINT IN WATER

Measure your horizon line and mark it on all three sides of the furniture. On this piece, the horizon line is 7½ inches (19cm) from the bottom of the dresser. Block in the water with one coat of Deep Midnight Blue and the ¾-inch (19mm) flat and let dry. Be sure to paint all the way around the three sides of the piece.

Add a second coat of Deep Midnight Blue, this time picking up Black with the color in some areas for shadow. Also pick up some White with the Deep Midnight Blue to add highlights. The water is slightly darker at the top and lightens a bit as it approaches the beach. Use the chisel edge of the brush to blend in some horizontal ripples with White.

Make the horizon line crisp by outlining it with a no. 0 liner loaded with thinned Deep Midnight Blue and White.

tip Often the shape of the piece will dictate where your horizon falls. You can use the bottom of a drawer, a cupboard or another element as your horizon. Just make sure the piece looks balanced.

4

ADD STRIPES TO LIGHTHOUSE

4 Sketch the diagonal stripes onto the lighthouse. Use the ¾-inch (19mm) flat to block in the stripes with Deep Midnight Blue. Use the chisel edge of the brush to outline the stripes and then use the flat of the brush to fill in with color. Let dry.

Shade all the blue areas on the lighthouse with Deep Midnight Blue and a touch of Black double loaded on a ½-inch (13mm) flat. The areas are darker toward the bottom and lighter toward the top. All your shading strokes should be curved to follow the roundness of the lighthouse. The stripes are lighter in the centers and darker toward the edges.

Add highlights to the blue areas with Deep Midnight Blue and a touch of White double loaded on a ½-inch (13mm) flat.

5

DETAIL RED AREAS

5 Shade the red areas with a ¾-inch (19mm) flat double loaded with Barn Red and Black. Shade the right side of the door. The area between the light and the collar is shaded on both the top and the bottom. Add a highlight in the middle with the ¾-inch (19mm) flat double loaded with Barn Red and White. Also highlight the left side of the door.

6

DETAIL GLOBE

6 Use Black and White and a ¾-inch (19mm) flat to shade the globe. It is darker on the sides and under the lip of the blue roof and lighter in the center.

Create the glow by blending some Old Parchment into the wet White in the middle of the globe.

Use the no. 0 liner and thinned Black to add the glass panes on the globe and the railings above the blue collar.

7 ADD WINDOWS, DETAIL DOOR

Paint the windows with a ¾-inch (19mm) flat double loaded with Black and a little bit of White. Once you've placed the windows, outline them with Black and the no. 0 liner so the edges are crisp. Make the left sides of the windows lighter than the right sides.

Use a no. 10 flat to paint the panels on the door. Start by double loading the chisel of the brush with Barn Red and a touch of Black. Make four *L* shapes on the door for the shaded sides of the panels. Clean the brush and double load the chisel with Barn Red and White. Make four *7* shapes connected with the *L*'s to complete the rectangle for the panels. You now have two shaded sides (the left and bottom) and two highlighted sides (the top and right).

The door handle is Country Tan placed with a no. 0 liner. Make a small comma shape for the handle.

8 PAINT SAND

Basecoat the sand with Country Tan and the 1-inch (25mm) flat. Add a second coat of Country Tan to the sand, this time picking up some Burnt Umber in the brush toward the bottom of the sand. As you move up, pick up some White with the Country Tan so the sand fades from dark to light. Create some horizontal marks with the chisel edge of the brush and Burnt Umber to give the sand some texture.

Spatter the sand with thinned Burnt Umber and a stencil brush (see page 14).

9 ADD SHRUBBERY

Use a small natural sea sponge to paint the shrubs around the lighthouse. The shrubs are placed between the water and the sand to hide that transition. Double load the sponge with English Ivy Green and Black and dab on the dark foliage first.

Go over the foliage with Old Parchment to add highlights. The yellow will mix with the greens on the surface and soften. The highlights should go on the top of the bushes to create form and shape within the dark areas.

10 PLACE SOME BEACH GRASS

Use a no. 4 round to paint some grass on the beach. Place dark blades first. They are a double load of English Ivy Green and Black. Use short, vertical strokes and vary their heights. Let up on the pressure you apply to the brush as you reach the end of the stroke so the grass tapers.

Add lighter blades with English Ivy Green and Old Parchment. Place the lighter blades on top of the darker.

11 SHADE SAND

Use a no. 8 round to float Burnt Umber beneath the grass and in areas along the beach to show dips and valleys in the sand. The paint should be thinned; wiggle the paint out to blend it into the sand around it. Also add some shading to the sand beneath the lighthouse.

12 ADD CLOUDS

Add the clouds with a natural sea sponge following the instructions on page 15. The more damp your sponge, the lighter and more subtle your clouds. Make sure the edges of your clouds are wispy and irregular like natural clouds. Don't make them thick and uniform in shape.

Use this same technique to paint the clouds on the top of the piece.

Load a no. 0 liner with thinned Black and make subtle *V*'s in the sky to represent distant seagulls.

THE FINISHED LIGHTHOUSE JEWELRY ARMOIRE

ABOVE: The front of the finished jewelry armoire.

TOP LEFT: The top of the finished jewelry armoire.

FAR LEFT: The left side of the finished jewelry armoire.

LEFT: The right side of the finished jewelry armoire.

This dresser captures a day at the beach with details that are fun and easy to paint. I love the warm colors of the umbrella, beach towel and tiny flamingo against the cool background of the sky and water. The dresser design is wrapped around all three sides, providing a unique view from any angle. And don't forget to add the nautical drawer pulls!

For the mural, you will learn how to paint palm trees with just a few brushstrokes and a sponge, and I will show you a technique for transferring lettering. You can also personalize the beach sign any way you wish. Place your dresser in front of a painted palm tree and beach sign, and your setting will be a sunny spot to relax!

life's a beach

materials

For the Beach-Scene Wall Mural

BRUSHES
1-inch (25mm) flat, No. 10 flat, No. 0 liner, No. 8 round, Stencil brush

PALETTE
Apple Barrel Acrylics: Black, Country Tan, English Ivy Green, White

DecoArt Americana Acrylics: Canyon Orange, Cocoa

Delta Ceramcoat Acrylics: Burnt Umber, Butter Cream, Old Parchment

OTHER MATERIALS
Carbon transfer paper, Cloud Sponge by Plaid, Painter's tape, Straightedge

For the Beach Dresser

BRUSHES
1-inch (25mm) flat, No. 10 flat, No. 0 liner, No. 4 round, Stencil brush

PALETTE
Apple Barrel Acrylics: Barn Red, Black, Country Tan, English Ivy Green, White

DecoArt Americana Acrylics: Canyon Orange, Celery Green, Cocoa, Deep Midnight Blue, French Mauve, Winter Blue

Delta Ceramcoat Acrylics: Burnt Umber, Butter Cream, Old Parchment

OTHER MATERIALS
2-inch (51mm) chip brush, 4-inch (10cm) foam roller

1

3

4

PAINTING THE BEACH SCENE WALL MURAL

1 BASECOAT TRUNK, SIGN

Basecoat the trunk with the Cloud Sponge loaded with Burnt Umber and a touch of Country Tan. (You are basically double loading the sponge as you would a brush.) Start at the top and drag down with the sponge. Apply a second coat of paint if needed.

Basecoat the signpost with Burnt Umber and Country Tan, double loaded on the sponge so that the post is lighter than the tree trunk. Use the sponge to place the edges and then fill in with a 1-inch (25mm) flat.

Basecoat the sign with White using the 1-inch (25mm) flat. As you move to the bottom of the sign, pick up a little bit of Black to create a dirty white for shadow.

2 BASECOAT SAND

For the sand, load the Cloud Sponge with Country Tan and pick up some Burnt Umber on the edge. Place the top edge of the sand, keeping the Burnt Umber at the top, and then work down, scrubbing the color in as you go. As you work down, apply less pressure so the sand color fades into the wall.

Basecoat the starfish with Cocoa and Canyon Orange, using a 1-inch (25mm) flat.

3 ADD DARK LEAVES

Use the chisel edge of the 1-inch (25mm) flat to paint the palm leaves. Paint the dark leaves first with English Ivy Green and a touch of Black. Paint the centerline first and then pull strokes off the centerline to fill out the leaves. Make the leaves curve as if they are hanging. Lift off toward the end of your strokes so they taper off to points. Also give your brush a bit of a twist as you pull out from the centerline so the fronds are thicker at the base.

4 ADD LIGHT LEAVES

For the lighter leaves, double load the 1-inch (25mm) flat with English Ivy Green and Old Parchment. Use the same techniques used for the darker leaves in Step 3.

5 DETAIL TRUNK

Use a no. 10 flat and Country Tan to add *U* strokes to the trunk to indicate different sections of growth. Load the brush pretty thin so the strokes are almost transparent.

6 PAINT BEACH GRASS

For the beach grass, load a 1-inch (25mm) flat with English Ivy Green and a touch of Black. Load your brush, then dip it in water, then load it again with paint so the color will flow onto the wall nice and smooth. Start at the bottom and stroke up, using the chisel edge of the brush to create the blades of grass. Make some blades very tall so they go up the trunk a bit.

Add lighter grass, using Old Parchment with a touch of English Ivy Green. The colors will blend as you apply the paint to the wall, creating several shades of green.

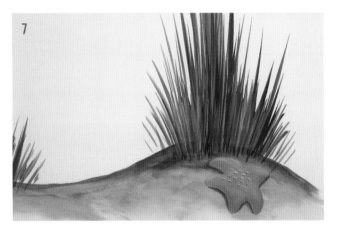

7 DETAIL STARFISH, SHADE GRASS

Use a no. 10 flat to add a little more Canyon Orange to the starfish. While the paint is still wet, add the highlights with Butter Cream. Place highlights on the top edges and left edges of the starfish. Also add some highlights in the center of the starfish. Make your strokes curved and flowing to follow the shapes of the starfish's arms.

Add Burnt Umber to the bottom right of each arm where they touch the sand. This creates a cast shadow that anchors the starfish to the beach.

Switch to a no. 8 round and paint the texture on the starfish with Butter Cream and Canyon Orange. Just push the brush against the wall to create bumps. Clean the brush and then pick up Burnt Umber and place this dark beneath each light texture mark you just made.

Clean the no. 8 round and mix Black and Burnt Umber. Water this mixture down. Float the color on under the grass and then wipe the brush on a paper towel. Return to the shadow to blend in and feather out the shading so there are no hard lines.

8 SHADE TRUNK

Use the no. 8 round to shade the tree trunk under the palm branches, again using Black and Burnt Umber. Use the same technique you used for shading under the grass.

9

SPATTER SAND
Use a stencil brush to spatter the sand with Black (see page 14). It's OK to get spatter on the starfish. This will create individual-looking grains of sand. To give the sand even more grit and texture, you can clean out your brush and spatter with White or a lighter color.

10 **TRANSFER LETTERING ON SIGN**
For the sign letters, select a computer font you like and print out a template. Attach the template to the wall with a piece of blue painter's tape. The sign is crooked, so the letters will not be level with the floor. Use a straightedge to make sure the letters are even with the bottom of the sign. Place carbon transfer paper behind the template and trace the letters. You can outline the letters or just place a line in the middle to follow for placement. If you outline the letters, be sure to paint all the way up to their edges so you cover the transfer lines.

11 **PAINT LETTERING, SHADE SIGN**
Use a no. 0 liner and Black to paint the lettering. Outline the letters first and then fill in the centers.

Double load a no. 10 flat with Black and White and place a gray line on the bottoms of all the jagged edges on the sign. Place a straight gray line across the bottom of the sign.

10

11

30

PAINTING THE BEACH DRESSER

The drawers on this piece are flush, so paint over all the divisions, treating each side as one solid surface. Basecoat the dresser with two coats of Winter Blue, using a 2-inch (51mm) chip brush and a 4-inch (10cm) roller.

1 BLOCK IN DESIGN

With a 1-inch (25mm) flat, basecoat the water with Deep Midnight Blue and add touches of Winter Blue and Celery Green in certain areas.

Block in the sand with Country Tan, Burnt Umber and Butter Cream, still using the 1-inch (25mm) flat.

Paint the palm trees following the instructions on pages 28–29, but use the no. 10 flat. Use the no. 4 round to paint the curves on the trunk. The tree in the wall mural and the trees on the dresser are identical, but with different scales. The trunk is Burnt Umber and Country Tan. The palm leaves are English Ivy Green, Black and Celery Green.

Use the no. 10 flat to paint the umbrella and the sun with Old Parchment.

2 PAINT THE PAIL, SHOVEL

Use the no. 10 flat to add a second coat of Old Parchment to the umbrella and the sun. Paint the pail with French Mauve and the no. 4 round. Add Barn Red for the dark areas and White for the highlights. Place the shading and highlights with the first coat of paint. The right side of the pail is lighter, and the left side is darker. Use a no. 0 liner to paint the handle.

The shovel is a mix of Deep Midnight Blue and Winter Blue.

3 DETAIL UMBRELLA

Paint the stripes on the umbrella with French Mauve and the no. 10 flat. Use the chisel edge to block in the area and then use the flat of the brush to fill in the space. The lines are curved because the umbrella is curved. Use two coats for full coverage.

The umbrella pole is White with a touch of Country Tan. Use the chisel edge of the no. 10 flat to paint the pole. Add a touch of this color to the top of the umbrella to show the pole going all the way through the umbrella.

Use the chisel edge of the no. 10 flat to add lines of Burnt Umber under the crescents of the umbrella.

Use the no. 10 flat and a wash of Burnt Umber to float some shading on the left side of the umbrella.

4 ADD BEACH GRASS

Add grass beneath the palm trees and at random spots around the beach with the no. 10 flat. The dark blades are English Ivy Green and Black. The lighter blades are English Ivy Green and Old Parchment. Make short, vertical strokes. Apply the dark color first and then add the lighter colors, letting the colors mix on the surface to create a variety of greens.

5 SHADE, SPATTER THE SAND

Float thinned Burnt Umber and a bit of Black beneath the clumps of grass with a no. 8 round and beneath the umbrella. Apply the paint in a line and then wiggle down to blend the color into the surrounding area.

Wet a stencil brush and blot off the excess water. Load the brush with Burnt Umber and spatter the color across the sand to create texture (see page 14).

6 PAINT STARFISH

Paint the starfish with a no. 4 round and Cocoa and Canyon Orange. Shade each arm with Burnt Umber. Highlight the starfish with Old Parchment and add texture bumps with Burnt Umber. Shade under the starfish with thinned Burnt Umber.

Paint the other sides of the dresser following the directions in Steps 1–6 where applicable.

7 BLOCK IN FLAMINGO

Basecoat the flamingo on the left side of the dresser with the no. 8 round and French Mauve, adding Barn Red for the shaded areas and White for the light areas. The darker areas are along the underside of the bird.

8 DETAIL FLAMINGO

Paint the legs Barn Red with the no. 0 liner. The beak is Black. Add a White highlight to the beak.

Use the no. 0 liner to dab on the eye with Burnt Umber and add a White highlight. Place a few feather strokes with Burnt Umber toward the bottom of the bird.

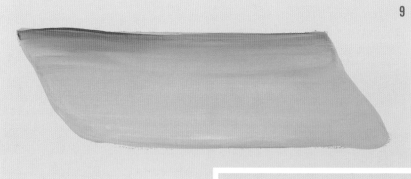

9 BASECOAT BEACH BLANKET

The beach blanket on the right side of the dresser is blocked in with French Mauve. Use two coats for full coverage. As you apply the second coat, add some Barn Red to the back of the blanket. As you get closer to the bottom, lighten the pink by adding White.

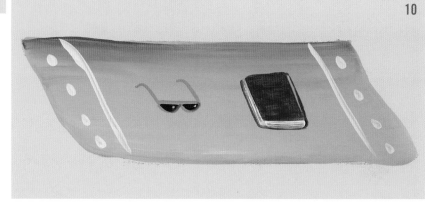

10 DETAIL BLANKET

Add yellow lines to the blanket with the chisel edge of a no. 10 flat and Old Parchment. Switch to a no. 4 round and add dots of Old Parchment to the blanket.

Use the no. 0 liner double loaded with Deep Midnight Blue and Winter Blue to paint the frames of the sunglasses. The lenses are Black with small White highlights.

Paint the book Barn Red with the no. 4 round. The pages are White. Shade the book a little bit with Burnt Umber in places.

Add tiny sailboats on the horizon, using the same steps shown on pages 18 and 19, but on a smaller scale.

THE FINISHED BEACH DRESSER

ABOVE: The front of the finished beach dresser.

TOP RIGHT: The right side of the finished beach dresser.

BOTTOM RIGHT: The left side of the finished beach dresser.

Transform a functional cart into a rolling flower stand with just a few overlapping pots and a variety of flowers. These flowers are a breeze to paint as you learn to double load a brush and overlap petals so colors can blend. You will have a well-stocked stand in no time!

These simple brushstrokes can create bouquets that are easily transferred onto the wall design as well. My favorite look is the crisp fern leaves against the texture of the basket weave. And adding a drop shadow will make these hanging pots jump off the wall. A garden setting like this would look great in your kitchen, mudroom or anywhere you want to create a garden nook!

flowers
for sale

materials

For the Hanging Baskets Mural

BRUSHES
½-inch (13mm), ¾-inch (19mm) and 1-inch (25mm) flats, No. 10 flat, No. 0 liner, Nos. 4 and 8 rounds

PALETTE
Apple Barrel Acrylics: Barn Red, Black, Country Tan, English Ivy Green, White

DecoArt Americana Acrylics: Celery Green, Deep Midnight Blue, French Mauve

Delta Ceramcoat Acrylics: Burnt Sienna, Burnt Umber, Butter Cream, Moss Green, Old Parchment

OTHER MATERIALS
4-foot (1.2m) level, Natural sea sponge

For the Flower Cart

BRUSHES
¾-inch (19mm) and 1-inch (25mm) flats, No. 10 flat, No. 0 liner, Nos. 4 and 8 rounds

PALETTE
Apple Barrel Acrylics: Barn Red, Black, Country Tan, English Ivy Green, Pure Silver, White

DecoArt Americana Acrylics: Celery Green, Deep Midnight Blue, French Mauve, Yellow Ochre

Delta Ceramcoat Acrylics: Antique White, Blissful Blue, Burnt Umber, Moss Green, Old Parchment

OTHER MATERIALS
Natural sea sponge

PAINTING THE HANGING BASKETS MURAL

1 BASECOAT BASKETS

Use the 1-inch (25mm) flat to basecoat the brown basket with Burnt Umber and a touch of Country Tan.

The basecoat for the white geranium pot is Butter Cream and White. Shade the right side of the white pot with a bit of Black and White to make a gray.

Sponge on foliage in the pots with a natural sea sponge and English Ivy Green and Black.

Basecoat the geranium leaves with a ½-inch (13mm) flat double loaded with English Ivy Green and Celery Green.

2 START BASKET WEAVE

Use the chisel edge of the ½-inch (13mm) flat to place a lip line around the basket with Burnt Umber and Black. Use the same brush and colors to create a checkerboard effect around the entire basket. Make short horizontal brushstrokes, alternating with a space between each stroke. The strokes are slightly curved as they go around the basket to show the round shape of the basket.

3 ADD TO BASKET WEAVE

Paint the light part of the weave with Country Tan and White, still using the ½-inch (13mm) flat. These light strokes go between the dark strokes you painted in Step 2. Tie the weave together with lines of the Burnt Umber and Black mix. Use the chisel edge of the ½-inch (13mm) flat to create the lines. Make sure the lines beneath the lighter squares are curved so the basket looks round instead of flat.

SHADE WOVEN BASKET

Float some dark shading under the lip and at the top of the lip of the basket, using watered-down Black and the ½-inch (13mm) flat. Also shade the lower right side of the basket.

Highlight the lip with Country Tan and White, still using the ½-inch (13mm) brush.

ADD DARK FERN LEAVES

Paint the dark fern leaves with a double load of English Ivy Green and Black. Use the chisel edge of a ¾-inch (19mm) flat to create the centerline of the frond and then pull out the sections of the leaf from the centerline. Your strokes should be curved, and you should let up on the pressure on the brush as you reach the end of the stroke so the stroke taper.

ADD LIGHTER FERN LEAVES

Paint the lighter leaves with English Ivy Green and Celery Green. Use the same techniques you used when painting the dark leaves.

7 DETAIL GERANIUM LEAVES

Shade the geranium leaves with the ½-inch (13mm) flat and a double load of English Ivy Green and Black. The leaves toward the back of the basket and in the center will be darker than the leaves in the front of the basket. The shading goes all along the bottom of the leaves.

Highlight the leaves with Moss Green. The highlights go along the tops of the leaves. Start at the center of the leaf and pull out and down in a semicircle pattern like that found on actual geranium leaves.

8 ADD VEINS TO LEAVES

Paint the veins with the no. 4 round and watered-down Moss Green. Pull the veins out in curved lines from the center like a fan. Also add a vein line around the edge of each leaf.

9 START GERANIUM BLOOMS

When you paint the flowers on the geranium, paint each bloom one at a time, taking the flower to completion before you move on to the next flower. The paint needs to be wet as you add each layer of color so the colors blend together on the surface.

Load a no. 8 round with Barn Red and place a bottom row of petals.

10 ADD TO GERANIUM BLOOMS

Double load a no. 8 round with Barn Red and French Mauve and add more petals. Make clusters of five-petal flowers, starting at the bottom of the bloom. Pull each petal into the same center point to make an individual flower and then move on and make another five petals beside it. The idea is to have the clusters overlap and mix together. As you move up with the blooms, begin to pick up White. Add more White as you reach the top of the flower.

11 DETAIL GERANIUM FLOWERS

Load a no. 4 round with Barn Red and dot in centers for some of the five-petal groupings. You don't need to dot in centers for every individual flower. Focus on the ones that are most noticeable, especially those toward the front of the flower.

Add the stems with the chisel edge of the no. 10 flat, double loaded with English Ivy Green and Black. You just need to connect the leaves and the flowers into the center of the pot. Make the stems slightly curved so they're not just straight sticks, and have some going up as well as down.

12 ADD CAST SHADOWS

Use a no. 8 round to float watered-down Black under most of the leaves and flowers. These cast shadows add depth and dimension to the plant. The shadows also should be darker in the center of the pot.

13

13 PAINT WIRES

Use a 4-foot (1.2m) level to draw a level line straight up from the middle of the pot. For this mural, I took the wire all the way up to the ceiling. Now draw two diagonal lines coming off the centerline for support wires.

Double load the chisel edge of the ½-inch (13mm) flat with thin Black and White and paint the wires. Keep the brush still in your hand and move your entire arm downward to paint a straight, continuous line. These lines should be faint and subtle.

tip When you are painting long sections that need to be straight and smooth, hold the brush still in your hand and move your entire arm. This will keep the brush steady, and your motion will be continuous and smooth.

14

15

14 START BUTTERFLY

Basecoat the butterfly with the ½-inch (13mm) flat and Old Parchment. Use two coats for full coverage. Use a no. 4 round to add a dot of Burnt Sienna to each of the lower wings. Clean the brush and load it with Deep Midnight Blue to add the wavy lines under the Burnt Sienna dots.

15 DETAIL BUTTERFLY

Load a no. 0 liner with thinned Black and outline the butterfly. Add the black markings on the wings and the antennae and paint the black body.

Place a White highlight under the eyes and on the body.

16

16 **ADD FINAL CAST SHADOWS**
Use a no. 8 round to float thinned Black along the
right bottom edge of each basket and the butterfly to
create a cast shadow on the wall behind each object.
Add a bee if you wish (follow the instructions on page
48).

PAINTING THE FLOWER CART

1 BLOCK IN DESIGN
Paint the wooden base Burnt Umber, Country Tan and Antique White, using the 1-inch (25mm) flat. Load the brush with all three colors and let the colors blend together on the surface.

Use the ¾-inch (19mm) flat to basecoat all the pots. For the silver cans, use two coats of Pure Silver. As you apply the second coat, add Black for the shading in some areas and add White for the highlighting in other areas. For the lines on the silver pots, paint a curved line of White. Then double load the brush with Black and White and place a curved line of gray directly beneath the White line to create a ridge both highlighted and shaded.

The geranium pot is Moss Green. The yellow pots are Old Parchment. The blue pot is Blissful Blue. Add Burnt Umber for the shading and Antique White for the highlights as shown for the green, yellow and blue pots.

2

2 ADD MOSS TO POTS
Double load a small sea sponge with English Ivy Green and Black and fill in the pots. Highlight this area with Old Parchment. This creates a mossy background for the leaves and plants to rest in.

3 PAINT LEAVES
Basecoat the leaves with a no. 10 flat double loaded with English Ivy Green and Celery Green. Shade the leaves with Burnt Umber and blend it in with the greens while still wet. The veins are a mix of Antique White and Celery Green applied with a no. 0 liner. Paint the geranium leaves following Steps 7 and 8 on page 40.

4

4 BLOCK IN ROSES

Basecoat the roses with Barn Red and the no. 10 flat. Let dry.

5

5 DETAIL ROSES

As you add a second coat of Barn Red to the roses, pick up some French Mauve to add dimension to the middle of the buds and White near the tops for highlights. Add some Black along the sides and bottoms for shading. The roses are darker at their bases.

Switch to a no. 4 round and add some detail lines to indicate individual petals and layers within the centers of the roses with Barn Red. Then apply some White to these lines for more contrast.

6

6 PLACE STEMS ON ROSES

Double load a no. 10 flat with English Ivy Green and Black. Place the chisel edge at the base of the petals and push in to create a teardrop shape for the base of the stem. Pull straight down into the pot with the chisel edge to create the stem.

7 PAINT YELLOW FLOWERS

The yellow petals are Yellow Ochre painted with the no. 8 round. Add Old Parchment to the darker bottom petals and White to the lighter top petals. Start with the brush at the outside tip of each petal and pull in to the center of the flower.

8

8 DETAIL YELLOW FLOWERS

Load a no. 8 round with Burnt Umber. Use a side curved stroke to place the center of each yellow flower. Underline each center with Black. Add an Antique White highlight. Load a no. 10 flat with English Ivy Green and Black and use the chisel edge of the brush to pull the stems into the pots.

9 PAINT PINK FLOWERS

The pink flowers in the blue pot are painted with Barn Red, French Mauve and Antique White, using a no. 8 round. Load all three colors onto the brush at the same time and pull in five petals to create each bloom. Some flowers will be darker, and others will be lighter, depending on how you load the brush; that's OK because you want some color variation in these flowers. The centers are Old Parchment dotted on with the no. 8 round. Underline the centers with Barn Red and the no. 0 liner.

Because you are using the same colors and brush, go ahead and paint the geraniums following the instructions in Steps 9–12 on page 40 and 41.

Load a no. 0 liner with thin English Ivy Green and paint the curling tendrils around the pot. Continue to add water to the paint so it flows on nicely. Add a few stems to the pink flowers as well.

9

tip The more flowers you overlap and add to the pots, the fuller they will look.

10 ADD BLUE FLOWERS

The blue flowers are like violets. They have two petals on the top and three on the bottom. Double load a no. 8 round with Deep Midnight Blue and Blissful Blue so your colors are varied. The double load gives the petals texture. For the centers, place three or four dots of Old Parchment in the middle with the no. 4 round. Accent the centers with Deep Midnight Blue. Add the stems with English Ivy Green.

11 DETAIL WOODEN BASE

With the 1-inch (25mm) flat, add some Burnt Umber and Black under the edge of the wooden base. Use the chisel edge of the brush to place horizontal strokes of Burnt Umber and Black to indicate wood grain and texture. Texture the lighter ledge with horizontal strokes of Burnt Umber.

12 ADD CAST SHADOWS

Float the shading with a no. 8 round and very thin Black (see page 13). Place the shading wherever pots are behind each other and along the base of all the pots so all pots look like they are behind the wooden base. Also shade on the cart itself behind each pot so the pot looks like it is coming away from the cart.

13 ADD BEES

Use a no. 4 round to paint the bee. The body is Old Parchment. Mix Black and White to make a gray and paint the wings. The head, stripes and antennae are Black and painted with the no. 0 liner. Also add vein lines to the wings with Black and the no. 0 liner. Add a White highlight to the head with the no. 0 liner. Don't forget to add a cast shadow behind the insects as well.

THE FINISHED FLOWER CART SIDES

BELOW LEFT: The right side of the finished flower cart. **BELOW RIGHT:** The left side of the finished flower cart.

14 PAINT AWNING (SEE FINISHED CART BELOW)

For the awnings, I used a plastic lid that was the size of the scallop I wanted, and I traced the bottom of the lid. The smaller the lid, the more scallops you will have. Paint the awning with Moss Green and a 1-inch (25mm) flat. You'll need two coats for full coverage. Float a cast shadow on the cart beneath the awning with a no. 8 round and thinned Black.

THE FINISHED FLOWER CART FRONT

BELOW: The front of the finished flower cart.

RIGHT: Detail of the top of the finished flower cart.

a shady seat

This bench has a lot of large, flat surfaces to paint, making it ideal for a mini mural. Not only do you have a view of birdhouses perched in tall grass, you have a great bird's-eye view of a pond on the seat! I will show you an easy technique for painting grass and give you some guidance on painting birds, frogs and other small creatures. Sitting on this bench will be fun as you enjoy the wildlife around you.

The tree wall mural sets the stage for the bench and repeats the grass, flowers and wildlife found in the bench murals. Because trees are versatile to a lot of mural themes, learning to paint a tree is a valuable skill. Give it a try as you create the ultimate tranquil setting and bring the outdoors inside!

materials

For the tree mural

BRUSHES
½-inch (13mm) and 1-inch (25mm) flat, No. 10 flat, No. 0 liner, Nos. 4 and 8 rounds

PALETTE
Apple Barrel Acrylics: Barn Red, Black, Country Tan, English Ivy Green, White

DecoArt Americana Acrylics: Celery Green, Deep Midnight Blue, French Grey Blue

Delta Ceramcoat Acrylics: Burnt Sienna, Burnt Umber, Butter Cream, Old Parchment, Straw

OTHER MATERIALS
Cloud Sponge by Plaid

For the bench

BRUSHES
½-inch (13mm) and 1-inch (25mm) flat, No. 10 flat, No. 0 liner, Nos. 4 and 8 round, Stencil brush, 2-inch (51mm) chip

PALETTE
Apple Barrel Acrylics: Black, Country Tan, English Ivy Green, Pure Silver, White

DecoArt Americana Acrylics: Celery Green, Deep Midnight Blue, French Grey Blue, Winter Blue, Yellow Ochre

Delta Ceramcoat Acrylics: Antique White, Burnt Umber, Mudstone, Old Parchment

OTHER MATERIALS
Large natural sea sponge, Scruffy brush

PAINTING THE TREE MURAL

1 PAINT TRUNK

Basecoat the tree trunk with a Cloud Sponge loaded with Burnt Umber and Country Tan (2:1).

Switch to a 1-inch (25mm) flat to detail the trunk. To shade the trunk, use Burnt Umber mixed with a bit of Black. For the highlight, use Butter Cream. Use a somewhat dry brush to apply the shading and highlights. The drier brush will create a scruffy texture.

2 ADD BRANCHES

Use the trunk base color and a 1-inch (25mm) flat to paint the branches. Let the branches vary in length and thickness so they look more natural, like real tree branches. Use the chisel edge and side of the brush to taper the branches.

3 DETAIL KNOTS

Highlight the edges of the knots (the limbs that have been trimmed off) with Country Tan and a touch of Butter Cream using a no. 10 flat. Place a bit of Black on the ridge of the knots for more shading. Add growth lines to the knots with the chisel edge of the no. 10 flat and Burnt Umber. These lines are just indicated; you don't have to give them a lot of detail.

4 PAINT LEAVES

For the leaves, use a ½-inch (13mm) flat. Place the dark leaves first. Double load the brush with English Ivy Green and Celery Green, picking up more English Ivy Green to make the darker leaves. The leaves are teardrop shaped. Start at the base of the leaf and stroke along one side. Then place the other side of the leaf the same way, ending in a point. Place the dark leaves sporadically and vary the sizes.

For the lighter leaves, double load the brush with Celery Green and English Ivy Green, this time using more Celery Green. Your lighter leaves can overlap the darker leaves in places.

5

DETAIL LEAVES

Use the no. 4 round for the leaf veins. On the darker leaves, the veins are Celery Green mixed with a little Old Parchment. On the lighter leaves, they are English Ivy Green. Start at the base of the leaf and place the center vein. Then pull veins out from the center.

6

PAINTING THE FENCE

The fence is 29 inches (14cm) tall. Each picket is 2¼ inches (64mm) wide plus ¼ inch (6mm) for the shadow. There are 2½ inches (64mm) between each picket. The angle at the top is 45 degrees. I used my level to find the angle for the top. The crossbar is 2¼ inches (57mm) wide with ¼ inch (6mm) for shadow. It's 4¼ inches (11cm) from the top of the pickets.

6 BASECOAT FENCE, PLACE GRASS, BASECOAT BIRD

Basecoat the fence with White. Use the Cloud Sponge so your lines are smooth and straight. Then go over the area with a 1-inch (25mm) flat brush to smooth out the paint and to paint the peaks of the pickets. Use the no. 10 flat for the gray shadows, which are simply a mix of Black and White. Hold your hand still and move your entire arm to paint the shadow so you have a smooth, continuous line.

Use the chisel edge of a 1-inch (25mm) flat to paint the grass. Use English Ivy Green and Black for the dark blades and Old Parchment for the lighter blades. Vary the heights of the blades. Let up on the pressure as you move your stroke upward so the strokes taper off. Add a slight curve to each stroke so the grass doesn't look stiff and straight. Remember to place some grass under the tree.

Basecoat the wren with a no. 10 flat and Burnt Sienna and Butter Cream. Add a bit of Burnt Umber to the top of the back. The breast is Butter Cream.

7 SHADE BIRD

Still using the no. 10 flat, shade the wren with a double load of Burnt Umber and Black. Feather in these colors with Burnt Sienna so there are no hard edges. Indicate feathers with lines of thinned Black, using a no. 0 liner. The highlights are a double load of Butter Cream and Burnt Sienna.

8 DETAIL BIRD

Use a no. 0 liner to paint the beak and feet with a mix of Burnt Umber and Butter Cream. Go back with Burnt Umber and underline the beak.

Paint a line of small vertical strokes of Butter Cream from the beak back to the neck, right through the eye area.

Paint the eye Black and add a dot of Butter Cream for a highlight. Outline the entire eye with Butter Cream.

9 PLACE FLOWER PETALS

Switch to the no. 8 round to paint the flowers. The yellow flowers are Old Parchment, with Straw added for the darker petals and White added for the lighter petals. The petals are longer at the bottom and shorter at the top. There's no set number of petals for this flower. Just use the width of the brush to work your way around the bloom.

The blue flowers are French Grey Blue and White. These flowers are smaller—five petals—but still use the no. 8 round. Pull the petals in from the outside edge to the center.

Paint the pink flowers with Barn Red and White, still using the no. 8 round. These are stalky flowers, and the petals make *V*'s stacked on top of one another. Place one stroke directly across from another to form the petals.

10 DETAIL FLOWER CENTERS

Continue to use the no. 8 round for the flowers. The centers of the yellow flowers are Burnt Umber. Use a curved, sideways stroke to place a shadow of inky Black beneath the centers and add a highlight of White.

The centers of the blue flowers are Old Parchment underlined with Deep Midnight Blue.

The stems on all the flowers are English Ivy Green, with a little Black placed with the chisel edge of ½-inch (13mm) flat. Pull the stems straight down so they fade into the grass.

11 ADD BUTTERFLIES

Paint the butterflies as instructed on pages 42 and 57. Feel free to choose your own placement and add as many as you like.

PAINTING THE BACK OF THE BENCH

Paint the entire back of the bench with Winter Blue using a 2-inch (51mm) chip brush.

tip When you apply the second coat of Winter Blue create some lightness in the sky by adding a bit of White to the top of the sky and letting it blend gradually as you move down. This is a subtle effect that gives the sky more dimension.

1 BLOCK IN BIRDHOUSES

Use the 1-inch (25mm) flat to basecoat the brown birdhouse with two coats of Country Tan. As you add the second coat, add Burnt Umber for shading and Antique White for highlights. These colors are streaked in; you can even turn the brush on the chisel edge to create some wood grain effects. Paint the post for the small birdhouse in the same manner.

Switch to the ½-inch (13mm) flat to basecoat the small birdhouse with Antique White. Add Burnt Umber for the shaded areas.

2 ADD ROOF TO SMALL HOUSE

Use the no. 10 flat to paint the stick roof of the small birdhouse with Burnt Umber, Black and Country Tan. Load the three colors on the brush at the same time. Pull downward with the chisel edge of the brush to create the small sticks. The colors will vary each time you reload your brush. Let the sticks overlap each other.

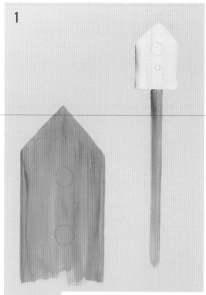

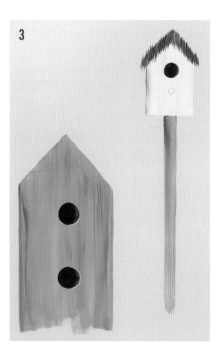

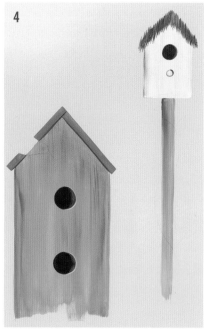

3 PAINT OPENINGS

Use the no. 10 flat double loaded with Black and Burnt Umber to paint the round openings in the houses. Use two coats for full coverage. Let the paint dry between each coat.

Create the inside edge of the openings with a curved backward C stroke using Country Tan and Burnt Umber. The edge is visible on the right sides of the openings.

Load a no. 4 round with Antique White and paint a highlight on the right sides of the openings.

4 PAINT LARGE ROOF

Add the peg on the small birdhouse with Burnt Umber and the no. 4 round. Paint a Burnt Umber circle and then soften the circle with Antique White so it blends. Then darken the right side of the circle by adding a little more Burnt Umber.

Basecoat the roof of the large birdhouse with French Grey Blue and a no. 10 flat. Mix some Black with the French Grey Blue and use the chisel edge of the brush to place a dark line along the bottom edge of the roof. Add a touch of Antique White to the top of the roof for a highlight.

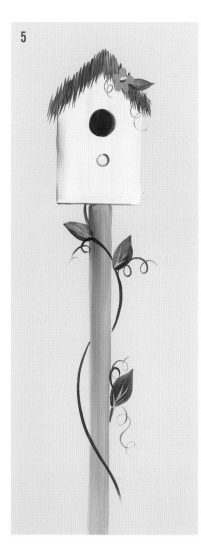

5

5 PAINT VINE AND FLOWER

Use a no. 10 flat to paint the leaves of the vine climbing the post. The leaves are English Ivy Green and Black. Add veins with English Ivy Green and Old Parchment double loaded on a no. 4 round.

Then load the no. 4 round with English Ivy Green and a little bit of Black and paint the stem. Let the stem curve around the post and connect all the leaves. Place the tendrils on the vine with a no. 0 liner and the stem color.

Use a no. 8 round for the flower. The petals are French Grey Blue with a bit of White. Start your stroke at the outer tips and pull into the center to create the petals. Place the center with a no. 4 round and a few dots of Old Parchment. Underline the center with Burnt Umber.

Also add a Burnt Umber underline to the bottom of the small house.

6

6 BASECOAT BUTTERFLY

Basecoat the butterfly with the no. 10 flat and French Grey Blue.

7 DETAIL BUTTERFLY

Use the no. 0 liner and thinned Black to outline the butterfly and add the markings. Add highlights to the eyes and body with White.

7

8

8 ADD GRASS, FLOWERS, WRENS

Paint the grass and flowers as instructed in Step 6 on page 53 and Steps 9 and 10 on page 54.
Paint the wren following the instructions in Steps 6–8 on pages 53 and 54.

PAINTING THE SEAT OF THE BENCH

9 PAINT SEAT

Use a 2-inch (51mm) chip brush to basecoat the entire seat with English Ivy Green. Then sponge moss over the basecoat with a large natural sea sponge and English Ivy Green, Black and Old Parchment. Use a scruffy brush to tap the color into the corners so you don't transfer paint to the other sides of the bench. Let dry. Sketch your design onto the surface.

10 BLOCK IN POND

Use the 1-inch (25mm) flat to block in the pond with Deep Midnight Blue. Add some Black for darks, and add washes of Celery Green and Winter Blue for color variation. Blend these colors with Deep Midnight Blue to keep the colors soft and subtle. The water is dark along the edges and lighter in the center. Keep a lot of water in your brush to blend the light and dark areas. Use the chisel edge to put in some thin, subtle ripples with Winter Blue. Keep the ripples light and don't use a lot of paint for them.

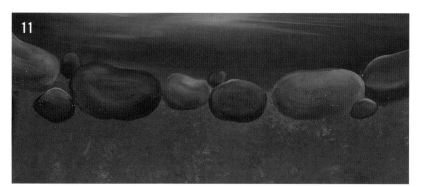

11 ADD ROCKS

Paint the rocks with the ½-inch (13mm) flat and Burnt Umber, Mudstone, Black and Antique White. Load the brush with all four colors at the same time. As you load the brush, use different combinations of colors to add variety to the rocks. Make some of the rocks browner by using more Burnt Umber and Mudstone. Make other rocks grayer by adding more Black and Antique White. Reload your brush as needed, but don't clean it between rocks. Let the colors blend together to create a variety of shades. Also be sure to vary the sizes and shapes of the rocks so they don't look uniform. Use irregular edges and avoid perfect circles and ovals. Use shadows and highlights to create form and edges within the rocks. Let dry.

Load a damp stencil brush with Black and run your finger over the brush to spatter the color onto the rocks (see page 14). Clean the brush and spatter Antique White on the rocks. Spattering the rocks will give them a great textured look, but try to guide where the paint lands to avoid too many spatters on the water and grass.

12 PAINT SNAIL

Basecoat the snail's body with Mudstone and Burnt Umber, painted with the no. 4 round. Use a no. 0 liner for the antennae. Paint the shell Yellow Ochre with a bit of Burnt Umber for the shading and Antique White for the highlights. Let dry. Use a no. 0 liner to add very thin lines of Black to show the spiral on the shell. If you don't get the spiral right the first time, that's OK. Just wipe the lines off while still wet or let it dry and paint over it with Yellow Ochre and try again. Use a no. 4 round to float Black under the snail for a cast shadow.

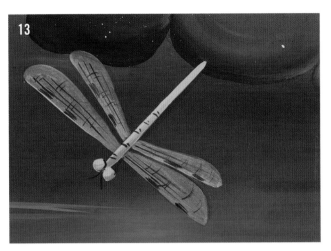

13 PAINT DRAGONFLY

Use a no. 4 round to basecoat the dragonfly's body with Winter Blue and some Deep Midnight Blue. Switch to a no. 8 round for the wings and paint them White and Pure Silver. Use a no. 0 liner and thin Black to add the detail and markings to the wings and body. Use the no. 4 round and Black to float a cast shadow under the body.

14 BLOCK IN FROG

Basecoat the frog with Celery Green using the no. 10 flat.

15 SHADE, HIGHLIGHT FROG

Use the no. 10 flat for the shading and highlighting on the frog. Shade the frog with English Ivy Green and Burnt Umber along the lower left side of the body. The shadow is particularly strong behind the rear left leg. Highlight with Celery Green and Old Parchment along the top of the back and on the head. Also highlight the top of the rear left leg so it stands out against the shadow behind it.

16 DETAIL FROG

Use a no. 4 round to paint the brown spots with Burnt Umber. Add a bit more English Ivy Green to the shading on the back as needed. Paint the eye with a no. 0 liner and Yellow Ochre and add a Black pupil. Add the nostril with Black. Then place a White highlight in the eye. Use a no. 4 round to float a Black cast shadow beneath the frog.

17

18

17 PAINT THE VIOLET LEAVES

Double load a no. 10 flat with Celery Green and English Ivy Green to paint the violet leaves. Let dry. Shade the leaves with Burnt Umber and highlight with Old Parchment. Add the veins with the no. 0 liner and Celery Green and Old Parchment.

18 ADD FLOWERS, TENDRILS

Double load a no. 8 round with French Grey Blue and White to paint the violets. These flowers are the same as the flower from Step 5. Pull five petals into the center to create the blooms. The petal colors vary depending on how you load your brush. Paint the centers with Old Parchment using a sideways comma stroke and the no. 8 round. Then add a Burnt Umber underline with a no. 0 liner. The tendrils are painted with the no. 0 liner and thinned Celery Green.

tip Remember, whenever you use the no. 0 liner, be sure your paint is thinned with water. The no. 0 liner is generally used for fine, continuous lines and the extra water will help keep the paint flowing from the brush.

19 ADD CAST SHADOWS

Add a cast shadow around each rock, both on the grass side and on the water side. Use a no. 4 round and thinned Black to float this shadow (see page 13).

19

THE FINISHED BENCH

TOP: The seat of the finished bench.
RIGHT: The front of the finished bench.

down the bunny trail

Create a sweet, playful setting by nestling bunnies on both a dresser and matching wall mural. I love the expression of the animals and how this theme appeals to both adults and children. You'll learn a great technique for painting fur and the secret to creating lifelike animals. (It's all in the eyes!)

The design flows directly off the wall onto the dresser by wrapping the grass, flowers, and butterflies for an uninterrupted meadow setting. Adding the insect drawer pulls is an accent that won't go unnoticed. Very cute!

materials

For the bunny dresser and mural

BRUSHES
½-inch (13mm) and ¾-inch (19mm) flats, No. 10 flat, No. 0 liner, Nos. 4 and 8 rounds

PALETTE
Apple Barrel Acrylics: Barn Red, Black, Country Tan, English Ivy Green, White

DecoArt Americana Acrylics: Celery Green, Deep Midnight Blue, French Mauve

Delta Ceramcoat Acrylics: Blissful Blue, Burnt Sienna, Burnt Umber, Mudstone, Old Parchment

OTHER MATERIALS
Painter's Touch Flat White by Rust-Oleum, 2-inch (51mm) chip brush, 4-inch (10cm) foam roller

1

2

3

PAINTING THE BUNNY DRESSER

Basecoat the entire dresser with at least two coats of white using a 2-inch (51mm) chip brush and a 4-inch (10cm) foam roller. I used Painter's Touch Flat White by Rust-Oleum.

1 BASECOAT BIRD, BRANCH

Use the no. 10 flat to basecoat the bird and branch. The branch is Burnt Umber and Black. The leaves are English Ivy Green. Double load the no. 10 flat with Burnt Umber and Burnt Sienna to paint the wings and back of the wren. Its breast is Butter Cream.

2 SHADE, HIGHLIGHT BIRD

Still using the no. 10 flat, shade the wren with Burnt Umber and Black. Feather in these colors so there are no hard edges. Indicate feathers with lines of thinned Black applied with the chisel edge of the brush. The highlights are Butter Cream and Burnt Sienna. Add a row of short brushstrokes from the back of the eye to the breast using Burnt Sienna and a no. 0 liner.

3 DETAIL BIRD, LEAVES

Use a no. 0 liner to paint the beak and feet with a mix of Burnt Umber and Butter Cream. Go back with Burnt Umber and underline the beak. The eye is Black with a dot of Butter Cream. Then outline the entire eye with Butter Cream. Give the leaves a second coat of paint, this time double loading the no. 10 flat with English Ivy Green and Celery Green. Leave some leaves darker than others. Add leaf veins with Celery Green and the no. 4 round.

4

BASECOAT BUNNY

Use a ½-inch (13mm) flat to basecoat the bunny with Mudstone, Burnt Umber and Butter Cream. Blend these colors together on the surface. Use Burnt Umber where areas will be dark (the lower body) and Butter Cream where areas will be light (mouth and chest). This helps model the shape so you know where to add shading and highlights.

5 ADD FUR TO BUNNY

Continue to use the ½-inch (13mm) flat. Use the basecoat colors to further define the shape of the rabbit and give the indication of fur by pulling your brushstrokes out with wispy strokes. Let the brush have a dry, jagged edge as you pull away from the body. You may need to wipe some paint out of the brush to achieve this effect. As you move up to the head, switch to a no. 10 flat. Continue to use wispy, jagged strokes to create soft fur. Create a bit of contrast on the ears to distinguish between the insides and outsides of the ears. Make lighter the bridge of the nose, the area above the mouth and the area around each eye. Use Butter Cream in these areas.

5

6 PAINT FACIAL FEATURES ON BUNNY

Switch to the no. 4 round and double load it with Burnt Umber and Black. Paint a defining line for the bunny's mouth. Line the ears with this color and add dark in the bottoms of the ears. Basecoat the eyes with this color as well. The pupils are Black. Mix Butter Cream and Black to create a gray and highlight the eye with a comma stroke. Start on the iris and drag the highlight into the pupil. Then apply a stroke of Mudstone under the pupil. Add some more Burnt Umber shading on the fur beneath the eyes so the eyes don't look like they are bulging. Paint the whiskers with thinned Black and the no. 0 liner.

tip To me, the eyes are the best part of painting a bunny or any animal in general. The eyes bring the creature to life and give it personality—a very rewarding step in the painting process! A great way to make the eyes seem more realistic is to mix a bit of gray and drag it as a highlight from part of the iris into the black pupil. This gives the illusion of a natural reflection. I sometimes also add a smaller white highlight next to the gray one for extra dimension.

7 PAINT GRASS, FLOWERS

Use the chisel edge of a ¾-inch (19mm) flat to paint the grass around the bunny. Use English Ivy Green and Black to paint dark blades and English Ivy Green and Old Parchment to paint light blades.

The yellow daisies are Old Parchment, painted with a no. 8 round. Pull the petals from the outside into the center of the flowers. The centers are Burnt Umber with a little Butter Cream. Float a little Black beneath the centers. Add a Butter Cream highlight each center.

The blue flowers are Blissful Blue with some Deep Midnight Blue. Pull five petals in from the outside to the center to create these flowers. The centers are Old Parchment. Underline the centers with Deep Midnight Blue.

The pink flowers are French Mauve with Barn Red and some White. These are stalklike flowers, and the petals make *V*'s all the way up the stems. Once the petals are painted, use the chisel edge of a no. 10 flat to place English Ivy Green stems up the center of the pink flowers.

8 BASECOAT MOUSE

Paint the grass following the instructions in Step 7. Basecoat the mouse with Burnt Sienna. The blade of grass the mouse is climbing is English Ivy Green.

9

9 SHADE, HIGHLIGHT MOUSE

Use the no. 10 flat to shade the mouse with Burnt Umber and Burnt Sienna. Use wispy brushstrokes with jagged edges to indicate fur on the mouse's back. This is the same stroke you used to create fur on the bunny in Step 5.

Highlight the mouse's back with Butter Cream.

10

10 DETAIL MOUSE

Use the no. 4 round to paint the ears, paws and tail with Burnt Sienna and Butter Cream. The color mixture is almost flesh tone. Place a little Burnt Umber inside the ear and at the nose.

The eye is Black with a Butter Cream highlight. Add whiskers with a no. 0 liner and thinned Black.

11

11 BASECOAT BUTTERFLY

Basecoat the butterfly with Blissful Blue and the no. 10 flat. Use two coats for full coverage.

12

12 ADD BUTTERFLY'S MARKINGS

Switch to the no. 0 liner. Outline the butterfly and place the markings with Burnt Umber. Highlight with Butter Cream around the eyes and on the body.

PAINT TREE
Follow the instructions on pages 52
and 53 to paint the tree on the left
panel of the dresser. Don't forget to
wrap some of the branches around
to the front of the dresser. Paint
the grass and flowers following the
instructions in Step 7 on page 66.

A detail of the finished bunny dresser.

PAINTING THE BUNNY WALL MURAL

The bunny wall mural is painted in the
same manner as the dresser, making
them a perfect match. They will look
terrific together, turning your room
into a little bunny haven!

To paint the bunny, follow Steps 4–6
on page 65. The wall-mural bunny is in
profile view but still has lighter fur on
its chest and darker fur on its back.

The butterfly in the wall mural is
identical to the butterfly on the dresser.
Follow the instruction in Steps 11 and
12 on page 67.

Paint the grass and flowers as you
did for the dresser following the instructions in Step 7 on page 66.

THE FINISHED BUNNY DRESSER

ABOVE: The front of the finished dresser.
RIGHT: The left side of the finished dresser.
FAR RIGHT: The right side of the finished dresser.

a day at the lake

Paint a scenic view by combining wildlife on a secretary's desk with a serene wall mural. Cattails grow around both lakes, and there's lots of nature featured, with a heron, a frog and deer watching from a distance. A fisherman on the drawer takes advantage of the peacefulness as he catches a tiny fish. I blended the drawer pulls for this project to avoid interrupting the scene on the desk.

On this project, you will experiment with blending as you create color variation in the sky, land and water. And by proportioning the elements correctly, you will achieve the look of depth in both scenes. Let the paint flow from your brush, using this cool color palette, and bring the calmness of nature into your room.

materials

For the Deer Mural

BRUSHES

1-inch (25mm) flat, No. 10 flat, No. 10 flat scruffy, No. 0 liner, No. 4 and 8 rounds

PALETTE

Apple Barrel Acrylics: Black, English Ivy Green, White

DecoArt Americana Acrylics: Celery Green, Cocoa, Deep Midnight Blue, Desert Sand, Winter Blue

Delta Ceramcoat Acrylics: Antique White, Burnt Umber, Mudstone, Old Parchment

OTHER MATERIALS

4-foot (1.2m) level, Cloud Sponge by Plaid, Natural sea sponge

For the Heron Secretary Desk

BRUSHES

½-inch (13mm) and 1-inch (19mm) flat, No. 10 flat , No. 10 flat scruffy, 2-inch (51mm) chip, No. 0 liner, Nos. 4 and 8 rounds

PALETTE

Apple Barrel Acrylics: Barn Red, Black, Country Tan, English Ivy Green, Pure Silver, White

DecoArt Americana Acrylics: Canyon Orange, Celery Green, Deep Midnight Blue, Winter Blue

Delta Ceramcoat Acrylics: Burnt Umber, Medium Flesh, Old Parchment

OTHER MATERIALS

Natural sea sponge

(Left) The Brisben Home

PAINTING THE DEER MURAL

1 BLOCK IN SKY

Use the Cloud Sponge to basecoat the sky with Winter Blue. Use circular motions to apply the paint. At the top of the sky, blend in some Deep Midnight Blue. Add White as you reach the horizon line.

2 PAINT WATER

Use the Cloud Sponge to block in the water with Deep Midnight Blue. Add a second coat of Deep Midnight Blue with a 1-inch (25mm) flat adding washes of Winter Blue and Celery Green in places. Blend in a bit of Black along the grass line. Use the chisel edge of the 1-inch (25mm) flat to add some ripples with thinned Winter Blue. Keep the ripples perfectly horizontal so they don't go uphill or downhill.

3 ADD FOLIAGE, GRASS

Use a small sea sponge to add the distant tree line. Start by loading the sponge with Black and English Ivy Green to create the dark foliage. Then add highlights with Old Parchment.

Use a 1-inch (25mm) flat to paint the grass with English Ivy Green, Celery Green, Black and Old Parchment. The grass is darkest where it meets the foliage and lightest at the water, so blend down as you go.

Once the grass is painted, add more bushes in the foreground with the sea sponge using the same technique you used to paint the distant tree line.

4 PAINT EVERGREENS

Use an old, scruffy no. 10 flat to tap in the evergreens. The evergreen are painted just like the distant foliage, but use the scruffy brush because it is a smaller area with a distinct shape. The left sides of the trees are darker and have more Black. The right sides are lighter with more Old Parchment. Place English Ivy Green in the center and feather the colors together so they are well blended. The trunks are Burnt Umber and Black painted with the no. 4 round. Shade under the trees with a no. 8 round and thinned Black.

5 PAINT ROCKS

Use a no. 8 round loaded with Mudstone and Burnt Umber to paint the rocks. Let the colors vary as you load your brush. Use Black for the shadows and Antique White for the highlights. Add Black along the bottoms and Antique White along the tops. The rocks in back should be darker than the rocks in front. Paint the rocks in the back first and then paint the rocks in front. Shade beneath the groupings of rocks with a no. 8 round and thinned Black.

6 BLOCK IN DEER

Basecoat the deer with a no. 8 round double loaded with Cocoa and Desert Sand.

7 SHADE, HIGHLIGHT DEER

Apply a second coat of Cocoa and Desert Sand, this time blending in some shadows with Burnt Umber and highlights with Antique White. Switch to a no. 4 round for smaller areas such as the legs and ears. I used more Antique White on the buck to make him lighter. The doe is darker and has more Cocoa.

As you paint the deer, let your brushstrokes follow the shape of the area you are painting. For example, use curved vertical strokes for the hindquarters and curved horizontal strokes for the bellies.

8 RENDER FACES OF DEER

Use a no. 4 round to shade and highlight the faces of the deer. Place strong shading on the left side of the buck's muzzle; then place a highlight on top of the buck's muzzle. This creates a strong contrast and gives shape to the face. Place some thinned Black along the ears and along the edges of the muzzles to define these areas more. Place Antique White at the tops of the eyes and at the tops of the muzzles.

9 FINISH DEER

The eyes and nose are a mix of Black and Burnt Umber painted with a no. 4 round. Add Antique White highlights to the eyes. The antlers are Burnt Umber with Desert Sand and Antique White. With the no. 4 round, add lines of Burnt Umber to the bottoms of the doe's legs for hooves.

10 PLACE GRASS, CATTAILS

With the chisel edge of a no. 10 flat, use English Ivy Green, Black and Old Parchment to place tufts of grass around the clumps of rocks and the buck's legs. Use this same technique to paint the cattails around the pond. Be sure to include the cattails growing in the water as well.

I added some rocks in front of the buck to help balance the shoreline. Paint these rocks following the instructions in Step 5. Place grass around the rocks.

Use a no. 4 round and Burnt Umber and Black to paint the heads of the cattails. Pull downward with the brush to make small, rectangular strokes. Use the no. 0 liner and thinned Mudstone for the stems and little pieces at the tops of the cattail heads.

Use a no. 8 round to float cast shadows under the tufts of grass, cattails and at the water's edge.

Use a no. 8 round and thinned Winter Blue to add ripples around the rocks in the water. Also place ripples around the cattails.

11

11 TEXTURE EDGE, IF DESIRED

I added a soft, textured edge to the finished mural to help transition between the wall color and the mural. Use the Cloud Sponge to apply this texture. The sponge should be almost dry and loaded with Burnt Umber, Mudstone and Antique White. Apply a little this mixture with a circular motion and then flip the sponge to the clean side and blend the color, removing most of it. Add more Antique White to the inside edge near the painting to soften the transition. Experiment with the color and texture until you find the style you like. You can make the texture as rough or as smooth as you like. This step is optional, if you like the look of a crisper edge, you don't need to add this texture.

PAINTING THE HERON SECRETARY DESK

1 PAINT SKY

Use a 2-inch (51mm) chip brush to paint the entire piece Winter Blue. In the second coat of Winter Blue, add Deep Midnight Blue to the sky section. As you blend in the darker blue, keep the brush damp and the paint flowing to help blend the colors together. You may have to experiment a bit with the color and blending to get the color just right on all sides of the dresser. The inside of the compartments are predominantly Deep Midnight Blue.

2 DETAIL WATER

The water is primarily Winter Blue with strokes of Deep Midnight Blue, Celery Green and White for texture. Use the 1-inch (25mm) flat to add these colors to the water.

3 PAINT GRASS, FOLIAGE

Use a 1-inch (25mm) flat to paint the grassy areas. Use English Ivy Green, Black and Old Parchment for the grass. The upper section of grass is lighter toward the sky and darker toward the water. On the lower side of the pond, the grass is darker along the water's edge and lighter as it reaches the bottom of the desk.

Use a natural sea sponge to pounce foliage along the horizon line. The foliage is the same color as the grass. Start with a base of English Ivy Green and Black and then add highlights with Old Parchment.

The evergreens are placed using the foliage technique and color, but created with a scruffy no. 10 flat instead of the sea sponge. The trunks are Burnt Umber and Black placed with the no. 8 round.

4 BLOCK IN HERON

Basecoat the heron with White and a ½-inch (13mm) flat. You may need two coats for better coverage. Use the no. 10 flat to paint the bill and the legs Canyon Orange.

5 SHADE HERON

Double load the ½-inch (13mm) flat with Black and White to make a gray and shade the feathers. Use the chisel edge of the brush to indicate feathers and make the gray a bit dark by picking up more Black in these areas.

6 ADD MORE FEATHERS

Add some Burnt Umber and Old Parchment to the feathers. Continue to use the chisel edge of the brush to create distinct feathers. These lighter feather lines are placed higher on the back wings. Then go over all the feather lines with White to soften them in places.

7 DETAIL HEAD, BEAK, LEGS

Use the no. 4 round to paint the Black feathers on the head. Paint the eye with two coats of Old Parchment. In the second coat, add some Burnt Umber to darken the eye. The pupil is Black. Outline the eye with a gray mixture of Black and White. Add a White highlight to the eye.

With the no. 10 flat, shade the beak and legs with Canyon Orange and Burnt Umber. The lower half of the beak is darker than the top. The left sides of the legs are darker than the right sides. Use Old Parchment for highlights.

tip   Remember, the fisherman and boat are off in the distance, so they will be quite a bit smaller and higher up in the scene than the heron.

8 ADD BOAT, FISHERMAN

Basecoat the fishing boat with two coats of Pure Silver and the no. 4 round. Add Black to the second coat for dark areas and highlight with White. Outline the top of the boat with Black.

Still using the no. 4 round, add the fisherman's pants with Deep Midnight Blue. His vest and hat are Country Tan. The sleeves are Barn Red. His face and hands are Medium Flesh, and his hair is Burnt Umber.

Use a no. 0 liner and thin Burnt Umber to indicate some features. Place a line of Burnt Umber down the vest and along his arms to separate them from his body and place a band of Burnt Umber on his hat.

Use the no. 0 liner to paint the fishing pole and line Burnt Umber with a bit of Black. The fish is Canyon Orange. Use Burnt Umber for the fins, gills and eye.

9 PAINT CATTAILS

Use the no. 10 flat to basecoat the cattails with Burnt Umber. Shade down the left side with Black. Blend the Black with Burnt Umber in the center and add Country Tan on the right side for a highlight.

The stems are Country Tan and Burnt Umber painted with the chisel edge of the no. 10 flat. Hold your hand still and move your entire arm to create smooth, straight lines.

10 ADD CATTAIL LEAVES

Add leaves on the cattails with the ¾-inch (19mm) flat. Use English Ivy Green and Black for the dark leaves and then place lighter leaves with Old Parchment on the top. Pull up straight on the chisel edge of the brush to make most of the leaves. For the bent leaf, start by pulling up straight and then twist the brush downward.

Also add some very short cattails to the distant shoreline.

11 PAINT SWAN

Basecoat the swan on the right side of the dresser with two coats of White using the no. 4 round. As you apply the second coat, add Burnt Umber and Black on the bird's tail feathers and on the side of its body. Use a Burnt Umber and Black mix to define between the feathers

on the wings, the legs and the beak. Switch to the no. 0 liner and add the eye with Burnt Umber.

Add the ripples in the water behind the bird with thin Deep Midnight Blue and the no. 4 round. Indicate some splashes with White. Go back and add these ripple and splashing details around the fish, fishing boat and distant shoreline as well.

12 PAINT FROG, DRAGONFLY

Paint the frog and the dragonfly on the left side of the dresser following the instructions on page 59. Add clouds following the instructions on page 15.

THE FINISHED HERON SECRETARY DESK

ABOVE: The front of the heron secretary desk.

FAR LEFT: The left side of the heron secretary desk.

LEFT: The right side of the heron secretary desk.

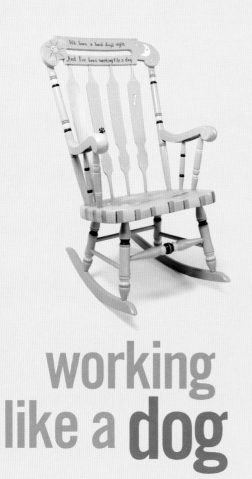

This nursery setting is a nod to tired, hard-working mothers. Every nursery needs a rocking chair, so why not paint it with the same charm as your nursery theme? I will show you how to master lettering with a liner brush and repeat the same dog character throughout the various murals. Watch the dog play in the daytime and sleep under the stars in trompe l'oeil windows. I love how the clock looks on the windowsill as it reminds you how quickly the days of childhood pass. The quote on the rocker sums up the life of a new mother; it ties the entire room theme together.

working
like a dog

materials

For the Rocking Chair

BRUSHES
2-inch (51mm) chip brush, 1-inch (25mm) flat, No. 10 flat, No. 0 liner, Nos. 4 and 8 rounds

PALETTE
Apple Barrel Acrylics: Barn Red, Black, Country Tan, English Ivy Green, White

DecoArt Americana Acrylics: Canyon Orange, Celery Green, Deep Midnight Blue, Winter Blue

Delta Ceramcoat Acrylics: Burnt Umber, Old Parchment

OTHER MATERIALS
Carbon transfer paper, Level, Natural sea sponge, Painter's tape, Red chalk pastel, Scruffy brush

For the Window Murals

BRUSHES
½-inch (13mm), ¾-inch (19mm) and 1-inch (25mm) flats, No. 10 flat, No. 0 liner, No. 4 round

PALETTE
Apple Barrel Acrylics: Barn Red, Black, Country Tan, English Ivy Green, White

DecoArt Americana Acrylics: Canyon Orange, Celery Green, Deep Midnight Blue, Winter Blue

Delta Ceramcoat Acrylics: Burnt Sienna, Burnt Umber, Metallic Gold, Old Parchment

OTHER MATERIALS
Natural sea sponge, Red chalk pastel, Scruffy brush

1 BLOCK IN DESIGN ON CHAIR'S SEAT

Paint the entire rocking chair with two coats of Winter Blue using a 2-inch (51mm) chip brush. Once dry, use a no. 10 flat and no. 4 round to basecoat the dog with White and Burnt Umber. Use two coats of White for the body. The bone also is White. The ball and collar are Barn Red, and the butterfly is Old Parchment. The mounds of dirt under the dog are Burnt Umber. To create the mounds, float on a line of the color and then blend it out so it fades.

2 SHADE WHITE AREAS ON DOG

Shade the dog with Burnt Umber and White still using the no. 10 flat and no. 4 round. Most of the shading is placed on the left side and underbelly. The shading is very subtle.

3 SHADE DARK AREAS ON DOG

Switch to a no. 8 round. Shade the brown markings on the dog's face with Burnt Umber and Black. Add more Black where you need strong shading. Add a little White to the tops of the ears for highlight. Add the brown markings on the back with Burnt Umber.

4 DETAIL DOG'S FACE

Load a no. 4 round with Burnt Umber and Black and paint the nails on the dog's paws. The eyes and nose are Black. Use the no. 0 liner to add a line of Burnt Umber and Black for the mouth. Also add eyebrows with Burnt Umber and Black. Add a small stroke of Country Tan to the left inside edges of each eye. These strokes help indicate that the dog is looking away from the viewer.

DETAIL BUTTERFLY

6 Outline the butterfly and add markings and stripes with the no. 4 round and Deep Midnight Blue. Add additional dots with the no. 0 liner and Barn Red. The body is Burnt Umber.

SHADE RED ELEMENTS

5 Shade the ball with Barn Red and Black. Using the no. 10 flat, add a highlight of Old Parchment on the right side of the ball while the paint is still wet so the highlight blends in. Shade the collar the same way, but use a no. 4 round.

Once dry, add the yellow details to the ball with Old Parchment and a no. 0 liner.

Run a small, dry scruffy brush over a reddish/pinkish chalk pastel. Apply this color very lightly in a circular motion on the dog's cheek to add a rosy blush.

> **tip** I have found that the best way to apply a soft, rosy tone to cheeks is to use a dry, scruffy brush loaded with "dust" from a red or pink chalk pastel. The blush goes on softly, and you'll avoid clownlike cheeks that can be caused by using paint.

DETAIL BONE, ADD GRASS, CLOUDS

7 Outline the bone with Burnt Umber and the no. 0 liner. Add tufts of grass around the dog, bone and ball. Use the chisel edge of a no. 10 flat and English Ivy Green and Black for dark blades of grass. Add lighter blades of grass with Old Parchment.

Use a damp natural sea sponge and White to add clouds behind the dog. Tap on an edge of White and then turn the sponge to a clean side and blend the color out to soften the clouds (see page 15).

8 TRANSFER LETTERING

Select a font on your computer and print out a template. Transfer the lettering to the back of the chair using carbon transfer paper. Use a hand level to help you place the lettering on straight. Once you are happy with the placement, secure the template with painter's tape. Then place carbon transfer paper behind the lettering, tape it into place and draw over your lettering.

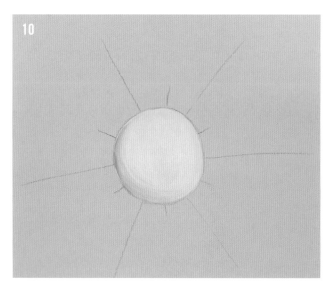

9 PAINT LETTERING

Use the no. 0 liner to paint the lettering with thinned Black. Make sure the paint is thin and flowing so the lines on your letters are smooth and even (see page 12).

10 BLOCK IN SUN

Basecoat the sun with Old Parchment and the no. 10 flat. Let dry. Shade the sun with Canyon Orange only on the left side.

11 DETAIL SUN

Paint the sunrays with the Canyon Orange and Burnt Umber. Use the chisel edge of the no. 10 flat. Pull the rays from the sun outward.

Use the no. 4 round to paint the facial features with Burnt Umber. The eyelids are Old Parchment lightened with White. Add small highlights in the eyes with the no. 0 liner and White. Add rosy cheeks with the chalk pastel and scruffy brush as you did on the dog in Step 5.

tip The placement of the facial features on the sun and moon can change their expressions and the feeling they give. You may want to experiment with where to place the features by sketching out the moon and sun in pencil and moving the features around a bit.

12 BLOCK IN MOON, STARS

Basecoat the moon with White and the no. 10 flat. The stars are Old Parchment. Use the no. 4 round to paint the smaller stars. Let dry. Shade with Burnt Umber along the back side of the moon at the top and bottom and along the bottom of the nose.

13 DETAIL MOON, STARS

The moon's eye is Burnt Umber painted with the no. 4 round. Add an eyelid with a dirty white made from White and Burnt Umber. The pupil is Black with a White highlight. Add the eyebrow and mouth with the no. 4 round and Burnt Umber.

Apply Burnt Umber to the left sides and bottoms of the stars.

Use the chalk pastel and scruffy brush to add pink to the moon's cheek.

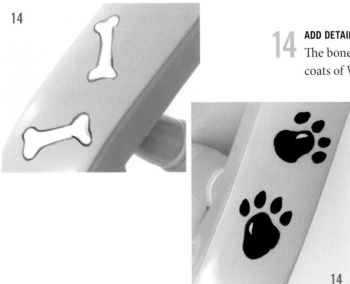

14 ADD DETAILS

The bones detailing the chair are painted with two coats of White. Outline them with Burnt Umber. The paw-print details are Burnt Umber, and all of these steps can be completed using a no. 4 round.

The accent colors on the spindles are Deep Midnight Blue, Old Parchment and Celery Green. The yellow detail next to the white dots is Old Parchment, painted with the no. 4 round. Use a 1-inch (25mm) flat for the stripes around the seat.

THE FINISHED ROCKING CHAIR

RIGHT: The seat of the finished rocking chair.

PAINTING THE WINDOW MURALS

Before you begin, decide how far apart you want to place the windows. I chose to measure from the corners of the room and make each window an equal distance from the nearest adjacent wall. Also decide how high you want to place the windows. Mine are 7 inches (18cm) down from the ceiling.

The windows are 31 inches (79cm) from the top of the arch to the bottom of the windowsill. The center window scene is 19 inches (48cm) tall with a 1-inch (25mm) frame all the way around.

From the top of the trim to the top of the arch is 4¼ inches (11cm). To sketch the arch, put a mark at the top of your trim and a mark at the top of your arch and draw a curved line downward to meet the edge of the side trim. Repeat on the other side to create a half circle.

The windowsill extends 2 inches (51mm) from the bottom of the scene. Add an additional 1 inch (25mm) for the front edge of the sill. The front edge of the sill extends 2 inches (51mm) beyond the edge of the window frame (1 inch [25mm] on each side). Mark off this extra inch and then connect a diagonal line from the corner of the window frame to the front corner of the sill.

> **tip**
> You can paint the window frame first, but it's easier to wait and paint it last. Then you don't need to worry about getting other colors on the trim as you work on the scene inside the window.
>
> It's faster and easier if you work on both windows at the same time. When you place similar elements, such as grass, bushes, trees and the dog, on a window, paint them on the other scene at the same time.

NIGHT SCENE

1 BLOCK IN SKY, GRASS
With the 1-inch (25mm) flat, basecoat the sky with Deep Midnight Blue with some Black near the top where the sky is darker. Add some very subtle highlights of Winter Blue toward the horizon.

Paint the grass with Celery Green, English Ivy Green and a little bit of Old Parchment. Blend these colors with a 1-inch (25mm) flat and allow some variation in the color.

The moon is White, and the stars are Old Parchment.

Paint the window frame White with the ¾-inch (19mm) flat.

2 ADD DISTANT BUSHES
Use a natural sea sponge to add distant foliage. Start by loading the sponge with English Ivy Green and Black. Then highlight this foliage with Old Parchment. The highlight should go along the top of the bushes and within them to add shape and texture.

3 DETAIL MOON
Paint the moon's face and details following the instructions in Steps 12 and 13 on page 87.

4 PLACE TREE
Basecoat the tree with Burnt Umber and the no. 10 flat. Add some Black for the darks and Country Tan for the lights.

5 ADD LEAVES
Double load a no. 4 round with Celery Green and English Ivy Green to paint the leaves. These leaves don't receive much detail. Let some be dark by adding more English Ivy Green and others can be lighter by picking up more Celery Green. Add veins with Old Parchment and the no. 0 liner.

6 BASECOAT, TEXTURE OWL
Use a no. 4 round to basecoat the owl. The wings are Burnt Umber. The chest is Country Tan. The face is Burnt Umber and Country Tan. Let dry.

Texture the chest with small strokes of Country Tan and White, still using the no. 4 round. Add a little bit of Burnt Umber between those strokes to add more texture.

Shade the dark areas with Black and Burnt Umber.

7 DETAIL OWL'S FACE
The owl's eyes are Old Parchment painted with the no. 0 liner. Add Black pupils. The beak is Black. Add White highlights to the eyes and beak.

8 PAINT DOGHOUSE

Use a ½-inch (13mm) flat and Barn Red to basecoat the doghouse. Use two coats for full coverage. On the second coat, blend in a bit of Black for the shadows and White for the highlights. The left side of the house and the right side around the door are shaded.

The roof and the opening are a mix of Black and Burnt Umber. Use the chisel edge of the ½-inch (13mm) flat to paint the roof. Highlight the opening with White and Burnt Umber. Use the chisel edge of the brush to paint the clapboard lines on the side of the house.

Place a Burnt Umber underline beneath the house for a shadow.

9 PAINT DOG, BONE

Paint the dog White and Burnt Umber following the instructions in Steps 1–4 on page 84. Use the no. 8 round to basecoat the body, and use a no. 4 round for the smaller areas and details. The bone is White with Burnt Umber details.

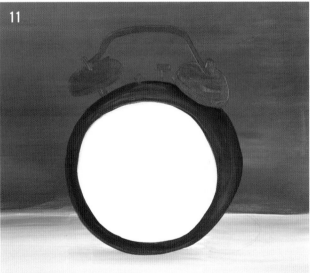

10 PAINT WINDOWSILL

Paint the windowsill with White and then shade it with Black and White double loaded on a ¾-inch (19mm) flat.

Now you can paint the trim around the scene if you haven't already done so. Use White and a ¾-inch (19mm) flat and shade along the outer edge with Black to make a gray edge.

11 BLOCK IN CLOCK

Use the no. 10 flat to paint the clock's rim Deep Midnight Blue and paint the bells Metallic Gold. Switch to the ½-inch (13mm) flat to paint the face White. The face will need two solid coats of White for full coverage.

12 SHADE, HIGHLIGHT CLOCK

Shade the bells with Burnt Umber and highlight with White. Use the no. 10 flat for most of the shading and the highlights. Switch to a no. 4 round for smaller areas.

Shade the rim with Black and highlight with White. Add the legs with Black mixed with a bit of Deep Midnight Blue.

Shade the face with the no. 10 flat double loaded with Black and White to make a gray. There is a rim of gray along the right edge of the face.

13 ADD NUMBERS TO CLOCK

Trace and transfer the numbers onto the clock. Use a no. 0 liner and thinned Black to paint the numbers. Also paint the tick marks. Make sure the paint is thin enough to flow off the brush. The second hand is Barn Red.

DAY SCENE

1 BLOCK IN SKY, GRASS

Basecoat the sky Winter Blue with a 1-inch (25mm) flat. Blend in some White as you get closer to the horizon line.

Paint the grass with Celery Green, English Ivy Green and a little bit of Old Parchment. Blend these colors with a 1-inch (25mm) flat and allow some variation in the color. Basecoat the sun with Old Parchment.

2 ADD BUSHES, SMALL TREE

Use a natural sea sponge to add bushes following the instructions in Step 2 of the night scene window on page 89. Paint the small tree as you did the larger tree in the night scene (see Steps 4 and 5 on page 90). Use the no. 4 round instead of the no. 10 flat for the trunk because this trunk is smaller. Use the no. 4 round to paint the flowers on the tree with Old Parchment. The centers are Winter Blue. Underline the flowers' centers with Deep Midnight Blue using the no. 0 liner.

Paint the butterfly with Old Parchment and the no. 4 round. Outline the butterfly and add some details with Burnt Umber and the no. 0 liner. The other butterfly in the mural is painted the same way but is Winter Blue and is outlined with Deep Midnight Blue. The body is Burnt Umber.

3 SHADE SUN

Shade the sun with Old Parchment and Canyon Orange using the no. 10 flat. Place a ridge of shading along the top edge of the sun and then blend the color down so it fades into the rest of the sun. Add some White to the center of the sun.

Double load the no. 10 flat with Canyon Orange and Burnt Umber and use the chisel edge of the brush to paint the rays.

4 ADD SUN'S FACE

Paint the face on the sun with Burnt Umber and the no. 4 round. The eyelids are Old Parchment and White. Place the back of the eyelid with the no. 0 liner and Burnt Umber. Add the rosy cheeks by running a dry, scruffy brush over a red chalk pastel and brushing the color on in a circular motion.

5 PAINT FLOWERPOT

The flowerpot is basecoated with Burnt Sienna using the 1-inch (25mm) flat. Let dry. Shade with Black and highlight with White, each blended in with the Burnt Sienna. The highlight is on the side closest to the sun—the left.

Paint the moss and leaves following the instructions on page 44. Paint the flowers following the instructions for the yellow flowers on page 46.

6 DETAIL GROUND, SKY (SEE FINISHED PAINTING)
Use a no. 4 round to add tufts of grass all around the murals as instructed in Step 7 on page 85. Also shade under all the grass mounds with the no. 8 round and thinned Black.

Add clouds to the day sky following the instructions on page 15.

7 PAINT WINDOW TRIM, ADD SHADOW (SEE FINISHED PAINTING.)
Paint the window trim White using a ½-inch (13mm) flat. On the second coat, blend in some Black with the White to define the edges with a bit of gray.

Paint a cast shadow around the entire window frame using thinned Black and a ½-inch (19mm) flat.

THE FINISHED WINDOW MURALS

If you are crafty and like to embellish, create curtains from fabric and mount them around the window murals with small hooks.

Create the taste of Tuscany with vineyard elements in this setting. I rebuilt the cabinet's architecture by painting columns around the paneled view of Tuscany's rolling hills. I will show you an easy technique for painting the grapes that accent the cabinet and the trompe l'oeil shelf above.

The painted shelf is perfect for that place where a real shelf is at risk of being bumped and is one you will never have to dust! Customize the wine bottle with your name or personal favorite and watch guests try to remove the painted glass for a taste!

tuscan villa

materials

For the Wine-shelf Mural

BRUSHES

½-inch (13mm) and ¾-inch (19mm) flat, No. 10 flat, No. 0 liner, Nos. 4 and 8 rounds

PALETTE

Apple Barrel Acrylics: Barn Red, Black, White

DecoArt Americana Acrylics: Desert Sand, Yellow Ochre

Delta Ceramcoat Acrylics: Antique White, Burnt Umber, Midnight Blue, Old Parchment, Royal Plum, Timberline Green

For the Tuscan Cabinet

BRUSHES

1-inch (25mm) flat, No. 10 flat, scruffy No. 10 flat, No. 0 liner, Nos. 4 and 8 rounds, Stencil brush, 2-inch (51mm) chip

PALETTE

Apple Barrel Acrylics: Barn Red, Black, Country Tan, English Ivy Green, White

DecoArt Americana Acrylics: Winter Blue, Yellow Ochre

Delta Ceramcoat Acrylics: Burnt Sienna, Burnt Umber, Butter Cream, Timberline Green

OTHER MATERIALS

4-inch (10cm) roller, Natural sea sponge

PAINTING THE WINE-SHELF MURAL

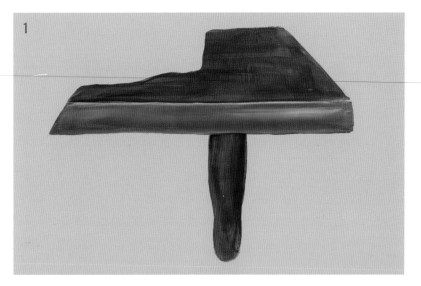

BLOCK IN SHELF

1 Load a ¾-inch (19mm) flat with Burnt Umber and Black and block in the shelf. Let the paint go on streaky so it looks like wood grain. For the second coat, add more Black to shade areas and add Antique White to paint the lighter areas, specifically the front edge of the shelf. Use the chisel edge of the brush to paint a line of Black along the front edge of the shelf. Clean the brush and run a line of Antique White beneath the Black line. Add more Black to the brackets of the shelf, especially in the areas where they meet the shelf.

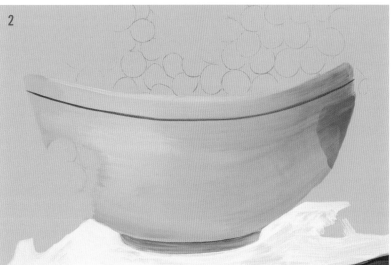

PAINT BOWL

2 Basecoat the grape bowl with Desert Sand using a ¾-inch (19mm) flat. Shade the bowl with Burnt Umber and highlight with Antique White. Add extra shading to the right side of the bowl where the grapes hang down. In this area add Royal Plum and a bit of Black to the Desert Sand. Add a stripe of Royal Plum near the top of the bowl with the chisel edge of a no. 10 flat.

Basecoat the napkin with Antique White and the ¾-inch (19mm) flat.

DETAIL CLOTH

3 With the ¾-inch (19mm) flat, shade the cloth with Burnt Umber. Add a bit of Black for the darkest shadows and blend them in with White. As you shade the portion of the cloth on the shelf, make your brushstrokes horizontal. Use vertical brushstrokes to shade the part of the cloth hanging over the edge of the shelf. Add highlights with White. Indicate a wrinkle by adding a shadow to the middle of the area hanging from the shelf. Then add highlights around this shadow. This keeps the cloth from looking too stiff.

Add stitches with Burnt Umber and a no. 4 round. Let the stitches follow the flow of the cloth. The stitches are just little dashes.

Add the shading beneath the cloth and where it hangs down with thinned Black and the no. 8 round.

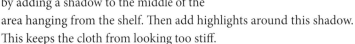

4 BASECOAT BOTTLE, LEAVES

Basecoat the wine bottle with Timberline Green and the ¾-inch (19mm) flat. The label is Antique White. The neck of the bottle is Desert Sand.

The grape leaves are also Timberline Green but painted with the no. 10 flat. Use the chisel edge of the brush to draw out the points on the leaves.

5 DETAIL LEAVES

Use the no. 10 flat to shade the leaves with Timberline Green and Black. The bottom left sides are where the shading is the darkest. Highlight the leaves with Antique White. The veins are thinned Timberline Green and Desert Sand double loaded on a no. 0 liner.

6 DETAIL WINE BOTTLE

With the ½-inch (13mm) flat, shade the wine bottle with Timberline Green, Royal Plum, Burnt Umber and Black. The bottle is darker on the left side. Use the no. 4 round for the neck of the bottle. The streaky highlights are Antique White. Alternate between shadow and highlight on the bottle to show the bottle's roundness.

Shade the neck label with Desert Sand and Royal Plum. Accent the label with Antique White and Yellow Ochre. The label is lighter on the left and darker on the bottom.

Shade the white label with Antique White and Desert Sand using the ¾-inch (19mm) flat. Highlight with White in the center.

Square up the right side of the bottle by running a line of Burnt Umber along it with the chisel edge of a ¾-inch (19mm) flat. Also run a line of Burnt Umber along the top and bottom of the white label.

With the no. 10 flat, basecoat the wine in the glass with Royal Plum shaded with Black.

7 ADD LETTERING TO LABEL

Sketch out the design on the label. Then paint the design with a no. 0 liner and thinned Burnt Umber. Remember that the label is giving you a three-quarter view, so any design should be off-centered, shifted to the right.

8 PAINT WINEGLASS

Paint the glass with very watery White with just a touch of Black to make a gray. Use a no. 10 flat for the overall shape. Remember, this is clear glass, so keep the paint pretty transparent. (You should still see your wall color behind it.) Use a heavier line of gray where you need a defined edge, such as the rim and along the edges of the stem. Then go back and pick up more White on a ¾-inch (19mm) flat to make the horizontal highlights. Use thin White to highlight where the top of the wine hits the side of the glass. Add shading at the base of the stem and at the neck of the stem.

9 ADD GRAPES

Triple load a no. 8 round with Midnight Blue, Royal Plum and Barn Red to paint the grapes. Start with the grapes in the back and work your way up to the grapes in the front. The colors will vary depending on how you pick up the colors on your brush. As you paint, don't clean your brush—just let the colors mix together. Try to make the grapes as round as possible, but it's okay if they're not perfect circles; the grapes are so close together that the edges overlap and cover any slight differences in shape.

tip Here's your chance to add a personal touch by customizing the label on the wine bottle. The label can be from your favorite wine, or you can personalize it with your family name and an important date in your family history.

tip

When you paint the grapes, work in small areas, taking the area to completion before you move on. This way, your paint stays wet enough to blend the highlight nicely. If you block in all the grapes at once and then go back to add the highlights, you may find some of the grapes are already dry.

10 HIGHLIGHT GRAPES
While the grapes are still wet, add highlights with Old Parchment. Put a backward-comma stroke on each grape.

11 BLEND HIGHLIGHT
Swish your brush in water so it's nice and wet and then blend in the highlight. Occasionally you'll get tiny open spaces between the grapes where the background color will show through. Fill in those areas with the grape color.

12 ADD STEMS, VINES
Load a no. 4 round with Burnt Umber and Black and add a stem to the bunch of grapes. Highlight the stem with Antique White. Add the curling vines and stems to all the leaves with the no. 0 liner and thinned Burnt Umber.

13 ADD CAST SHADOWS
Float a cast shadow around each element in the mural and around the shelf on the wall itself with a no. 8 round and thinned Black. These shadows will help nestle in the elements on the shelf and make the shelf look three dimensional.

PAINTING THE TUSCAN CABINET

Paint the feet, the top, the sides and the trim of the cabinet door with Country Tan. Use a 2-inch (51mm) chip brush and a 4-inch (10cm) foam roller for a smooth finish. Basecoat the columns with Butter Cream and the 1-inch (25mm) flat.

1 **BLOCK IN BACKGROUND**

Use a 1-inch (25mm) flat to paint the sky in the top panel with Winter Blue, blending in some White toward the horizon.

Paint the hills starting at the top and working down. The overall ground color is Timberline Green. Blend in some Yellow Ochre and White to lighten some places. Blend some Burnt Umber with Timberline Green for the darker areas. Apply the lights and darks to create the appearance of hills, valleys and general landforms. Remember to keep a good amount of water in your brush so the paint flows off it and blends well. Leave two open areas for fields. Paint these fields with Country Tan.

2 DETAIL FIELDS, ADD FOLIAGE, TREES

Shade the fields with Burnt Umber and highlight with Butter Cream. Use the natural sea sponge to pat on bushes and foliage with Timberline Green and English Ivy Green. The darkest areas of foliage have Burnt Umber in them as well. Add Yellow Ochre highlights to give shape and form to the bushes.

The conelike trees are Timberline Green and English Ivy Green painted with the no. 4 round. The trees are rounder at the base. Squiggle the stroke upward so the trees are thinner at the top. Shade the trees on the left with Burnt Umber and highlight on the right with Yellow Ochre.

3 ADD TEXTURE UNDER TREES, PAINT CROPS

Load a scruffy no. 10 flat with thinned English Ivy Green and Burnt Umber and add subtle texture to the base of the trees. Keep the paint thin so the texture does not become too distinct. Then pick up clean water with a no. 8 round and place the water over the texture so it blends and softens a bit.

Load a no. 8 round with Timberline Green and Burnt Umber and place small horizontal strokes in the fields to represent crops. The stroke is not a dot; it's a bit like a dash or blot. Under these random strokes, place a Burnt Umber underline with a no. 0 liner.

4 PAINT BUILDINGS

Use a no. 10 flat and Butter Cream to basecoat the walls of the buildings. Let dry. Shade the left sides of the walls with Burnt Umber. Also add shading where the buildings come together. Add highlights with Butter Cream. The roofs are Barn Red and Burnt Sienna. Use the chisel edge of a nice no. 10 flat (not a scruffy brush) for the roof edges. Use a no. 4 round to fill in any additional roof area. Add the door to the small house on the hill using the roof color as well. Underline the roof in places with Burnt Umber and the chisel edge of the no. 10.

Add the windows with Burnt Umber and the no. 4 round. The top window on the tower is Timberline Green and Yellow Ochre because there are two aligned openings on the tower that let the viewer see directly through the tiny building's walls. Define the edges of the windows with the no. 0 liner and thinned Black. Place the edges on the left sides and the bottoms of the windows. Also use the no. 0 liner to add the slate roof details on the bottom roofline of the long building.

5 ADD SCRUFFY TREES

Use a no. 4 round loaded with Burnt Umber and some Black to paint the trunks of the scruffy trees near the large building. Use the scruffy no. 10 flat to tap on the leaves with Timberline Green and English Ivy Green. Add some Burnt Umber for the darks. Highlight with Yellow Ochre. As you add the leaves to the tree, also add some scruffy foliage in front of the large building to hide the building's edge lines.

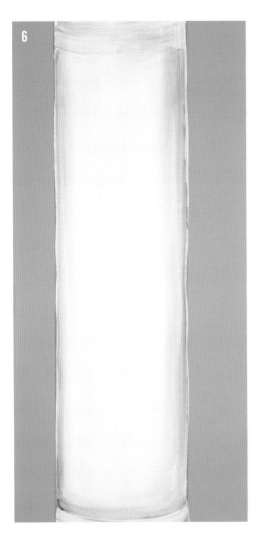

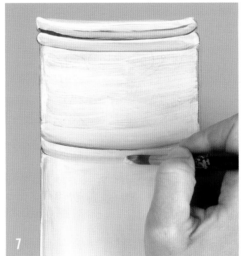

6 SHADE COLUMNS

Shade the sides of the columns with Burnt Umber using the 1-inch (25mm) flat. As you work your way into the center add Butter Cream for a highlight. This will show the roundness of the column.

7 PAINT TURNS

Double load a no. 8 round with Butter Cream and Burnt Umber. Use a curved horizontal line to paint the turn. Wipe the brush clean (but don't rinse it), pick up Butter Cream and go over the stroke again to soften and blend it.

9 DETAIL CARVED AREA

Use a no. 8 round loaded with Butter Cream to define the shapes of the carved areas more. Paint the raised sections of the carved area with this color. While the Butter Cream is still wet, add some Burnt Umber, starting at the base and working up so there is a subtle shadow. Add a line of shading at the bottom of the carved section with the no. 8 round and thinned Burnt Umber.

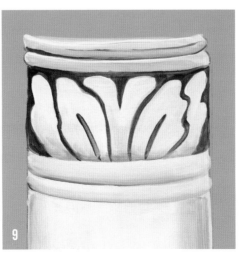

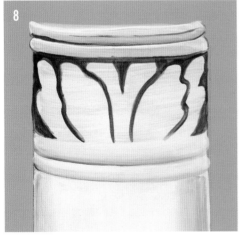

8 PAINT CARVING DETAIL

Double load a no. 8 round with Burnt Umber and Black and paint the darkness around the carved shapes.

10 **PAINT TRIM AROUND "WINDOWS"**
Paint the trim directly around the window areas with two coats of Burnt Umber. Load a stencil brush with Burnt Umber and spatter it all over the piece (see page 14). Clean the brush and load it with Antique White and spatter this color all over the piece as well.

11 **ADD LEAVES, GRAPES TO SIDES**
The grape leaves and tendrils are painted following the instructions in Steps 4 and 5 on page 99.

Paint the bunches of grapes on either side of the cabinet following the instructions in Steps 9–12 on pages 100 and 101.

THE FINISHED TUSCAN CABINET

TOP LEFT: The right side of the finished Tuscan cabinet.
BOTTOM LEFT: The left side of the finished Tuscan cabinet.
ABOVE: The front of the finished Tuscan cabinet.
BELOW: A detail from the top of the finished Tuscan cabinet.

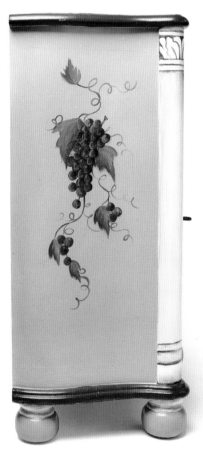

the brownstone

Bring bustling charm to your room with this apartment building and gaslight mural. The details on the brownstone include small hanging pots, a clothesline and sleeping cats in the windows. You'll learn how to paint these charming windows step by step, and then you can have fun filling them with whatever little surprises you choose. And don't forget the clever drawer pulls that look just like window awnings. The table and chairs set out front invite you to linger and enjoy the view long into the evening where a lamppost wall mural will light the scene. Make the lamppost jump off your wall with highlights and a cast shadow; the best part is having a street named after you!

materials

For the Gaslight Mural

BRUSHES
½-inch (13mm) and 1-inch (25mm) flats, No. 10 flat, No. 0 liner, Nos. 4 and 8 rounds

PALETTE
Apple Barrel Acrylics: Black, White

Delta Ceramcoat Acrylics: Metallic Gold

OTHER MATERIALS
4-foot (1.2m) level, Carbon transfer paper, Cloud Sponge by Plaid, Mr. Clean Magic Eraser, Painter's tape, Pencil, Long Straightedge

For the Town-house Dresser

BRUSHES
2-inch (51mm) chip, Stencil brush, ½-inch (13mm), ¾-inch (19mm) and 1-inch (25mm) flats, scruffy No. 10 flat, No. 0 liner, No. 4 round

PALETTE
Apple Barrel Acrylics: Barn Red, Black, Country Tan, English Ivy Green, Pure Silver, White

DecoArt Americana Acrylics: Cocoa, Deep Midnight Blue, Winter Blue

Delta Ceramcoat Acrylics: Antique White, Burnt Sienna, Burnt Umber, Old Parchment

OTHER MATERIALS
Cloud Sponge by Plaid, Natural sea sponge, Pencil, Small level, Straightedge

PAINTING THE GASLIGHT MURAL

The gaslight mural measures 75 inches (1.9m) high from the baseboard. It measures 3 inches (7.6cm) across at its widest point.

Use a long metal straightedge and a 4-foot (1.2m) level to create the straight lines of the vertical post. The first set of turnings is 19 inches (48cm) from the baseboard. The second set of turnings is 30 inches (76cm) from the baseboard. The arm is 17 inches (43cm) long and 1 inch (25mm) wide.

1 BASECOAT POST, SIGN

Basecoat the entire post with Black using a Cloud Sponge. Use a 1-inch (25mm) flat and a no. 8 round for the intricate areas. Basecoat the white sign with White using a 1-inch (25mm) flat.

2 HIGHLIGHT POST

Load Black and White on a 1-inch (25mm) flat and highlight the left side of the post. The colors mix together on the wall and create a gray highlight. Dip your brush in water occasionally to help the paint blend on more smoothly. Use vertical strokes.

Once you reach the center of the post, wipe your brush and pick up only Black to blend the highlight over toward the right side.

Switch to a no. 8 round. Double load this brush with White and Black and place the highlights on the tops of the turns on the post. Apply these highlights with curved strokes to show that this is a rounded area, not flat. Work your way down each turn and then wipe your brush and pick up straight Black to help blend the highlights. Shade and highlight the cap at the top of the lamp as well.

Remember, on the post you are blending the highlight from the left to the right. On the turns you are blending the highlight from top to bottom.

3 HIGHLIGHT SIGN ARM

Also use the no. 8 round to highlight the arm that holds the sign. Work from the top down, as you did with the turns, but use a straight line instead of a curved line. Highlight the ball on the end with a little stroke on the left side, just like the turns.

Be sure to highlight the top of the gaslight and prongs holding the lamp in place.

4

PAINT INSIDE OF LAMP

Use the ½-inch (13mm) flat to paint the light filament with White. Use two coats for full coverage and be sure to let the paint dry between coats. Use the chisel edge to outline the precise shape and then fill in with the flat of your brush. Dip your brush in water and pick up Black and White and paint the inside of the lamp's top. Be sure you have enough water in your brush to make this area washy.

5

5

DETAIL SIGN

Switch to a 1-inch (25mm) flat and apply a second coat of White to the sign. As you move down the sign, pick up a little bit of Black in the White to create a dirty white for shadow at the bottom of the sign. Keep your brush wet, picking up water as you go to keep the paint flowing and blending smoothly. Use the chisel edge of your brush along the edges to define the shape.

6

PAINT LAMP'S GLASS

Use a 1-inch (25mm) flat to put a thin wash of White wherever there are panes of glass. Go right over the areas you've already painted so it is transparent. Use straight, downward strokes. Add a second layer of wash if the first is too transparent, but be sure to let the paint dry between applications. The edges of the panes do not need to be crisp, as they will be covered with Black later.

6

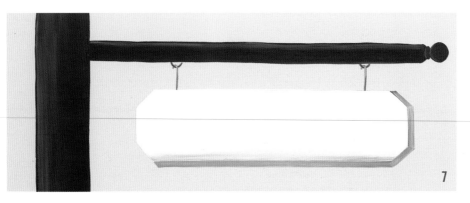

7

8

7 DETAIL SIGN

Use a no. 10 flat to paint a gray edge only on the right and bottom sides of the sign to create a shadowed edge.

Use the no. 4 round and Metallic Gold to paint in the loops and hooks for the sign. Paint the loops first and then the hooks. This will require two coats because the metallic paint is very thin and transparent. On the second coat, add a touch of Black and shade the loop parts so they are darker than the hooks. The loops are behind the hooks. Add shading on the hooks where they meet the sign.

Add a White highlight stroke at the tops of the hooks as they come out from the loops.

8 DETAIL LAMP

Load a ½-inch (13mm) flat with Black and basecoat the trim areas holding the glass panes in place. Use the chisel edge to define the shape and then fill in with the flat of the brush. Use two coats for full coverage.

As you add the second coat, you can add the highlights to blend them easier. There's not much highlight on these sections—just a White line. Don't blend. Let the color get picked up in the black paint and mix with the color around it. Place a highlight around the top of the center point so it has contrast with the black cap behind it.

9

9 TRANSFER LETTERING

For the letters, I selected a computer font that looked appropriate for a street sign—something bold and easy to read. I used Helvetica for this mural.

Measure a ½ inch (13mm) up from the bottom white edge of the sign and use a pencil to make a faint line where the lettering will sit.

Place one piece of blue painter's tape at the top of your template and then use the level to place the template so the lettering is level on your pencil line. Once the letters are level, tape the template in place and then tape carbon transfer paper behind it. Trace over the letters to transfer them onto the sign.

tip I have found that when I wipe over dried black paint to remove graphite transfer lines, the paint smears even if it has dried. To avoid this, I transfer only in the middle of the letters so paint will cover the graphite and the lines don't show. That way I don't have to worry about removing the lines and smearing the paint.

10 PAINT LETTERING

Once the letters are roughed in, paint them Black using a no. 4 round. Use a no. 0 liner to paint any tight areas on the letters. The paint should be thinned down a bit so the strokes flow easily. You only need one coat of paint.

Let the paint dry. Clean up any carbon smudges with a Mr. Clean Magic Eraser. Use a careful, light touch—no scrubbing.

10

11

11 ADD CAST SHADOW TO WALL

Using a no. 8 round, float a cast shadow using thinned Black along the right side of the lamppost. Paint directly up against the existing painting, right against the lamppost. The shadow should take the shape of the post. Also place the shadow underneath the arm holding the sign.

**THE FINISHED
GASLIGHT MURAL**

PAINTING THE TOWN-HOUSE DRESSER

Triple load the Cloud Sponge with Burnt Umber, Burnt Sienna and Barn Red. Cover the entire surface (except the top) with this color. Try to keep your strokes linear. Apply two coats and let dry.

Clean the sponge, wring out the excess moisture and load it with Burnt Umber only. Wipe this color over the entire surface in a variety of directions to give it a dirty feel. Let dry.

Load a stencil brush with thinned Black and spatter the entire surface (see page 14). Clean the brush, load it with White and spatter the surface again. This will give the building a brick texture.

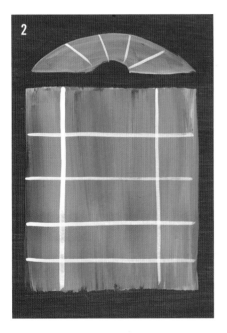

1 PAINT WINDOWS

Use a straightedge, a small level and a pencil to place the windows. Let the width and height of the dresser determine where you place the windows and how large they are. Mine typically are 3 inches (8cm) wide and 4½ inches (11cm) high.

Double load a 1-inch (25mm) flat with Black and White and let the colors mix on the surface to create a gray basecoat for all the windows.

If you wanted to use the knobs that came with the dresser or center pulls instead of awning pulls, you can paint arches in your windows. The step-by-step photos show you how to add those arches, but my finished piece has awning pulls.

Load a 1-inch (25mm) flat with Black and White and paint in the sidewalk on the piece as well.

2 ADD WHITE WINDOW GRIDS

Load a no. 0 liner with thinned White and add the window grids. The spacing of your horizontal grids depends on how tall you make your window, so the taller your window, the more divisions you will have. It takes a lot of practice to get the grids straight. If you're not happy with the line you paint, immediately wipe it off with a damp paper towel and try again.

3 ADD TAN TRIM

For the tan trim, load the no. 4 round with Country Tan and a little bit of Antique White.

4 PAINT BLACK RAILING

Load the no. 0 liner with thinned Black and paint the railing on the window. Paint a horizontal line first and then add six crossbars. Then fill in with wrought-iron scrolling.

Add any plant detail to the windows at this time as well. I often add hanging baskets. Load a no. 4 round with Burnt Sienna and paint a bowl shape; then shade with Black. Paint this right over the window trim.

For window baskets attached to the wrought-iron railing, load a no. 4 round with Burnt Sienna and paint directly on top of the rails. Shade with Black. Place a line of Black over it to attach it to the railing.

Scatter these elements throughout the piece. Don't place one in every window.

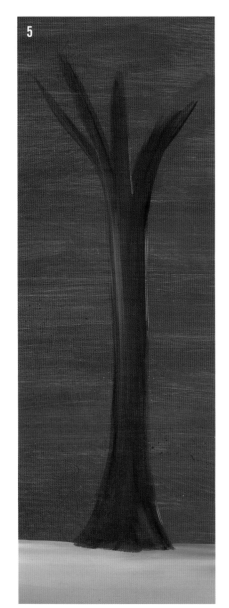

5 BLOCK IN TREE TRUNKS

Paint the tree trunks on the sides of the dresser with a ¾-inch (19mm) flat and two coats of Burnt Umber. In the second coat, shade with Black and highlight with Country Tan.

6 PAINT DOOR

Basecoat the door with English Ivy Green using the 1-inch (25mm) flat. Shade the left side of the door with English Ivy Green and Black and the ¾-inch (19mm) flat. Highlight the right side of the door with English Ivy Green and White. Let dry.

Load the ¾-inch (19mm) flat with Black and White and add a gray window to the top portion of the door.

Use the chisel edge of the ½-inch (13mm) flat to paint the bottoms and left sides of the door panels with English Ivy Green and Black. Make an L shape. Clean the brush and double load it with English Ivy Green and White to paint the tops and right sides of the panel. Make a 7 shape that connects with the L shape.

Basecoat the awning with Black using the ½-inch (13mm) flat.

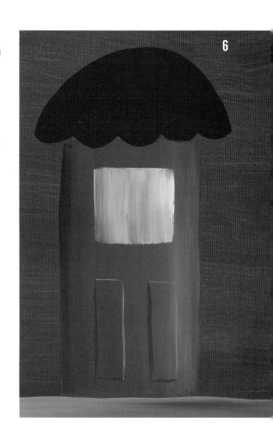

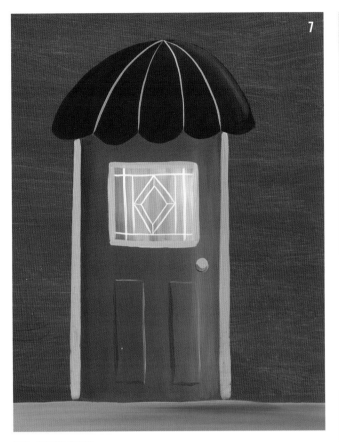

7 DETAIL DOOR

Load a no. 0 liner with thin White and paint the panes on the window glass. Switch to a no. 4 round, double load it with Country Tan and Antique White and add a vertical line on either side of the door. Add the doorknob with this same color. Place a line of Burnt Umber beneath the doorknob.

Add a very subtle highlight to the right side of the awning with the ½-inch (13mm) flat double loaded with Black and White to make a gray. Load this same color on a no. 0 liner and add subtle panel lines to the awning.

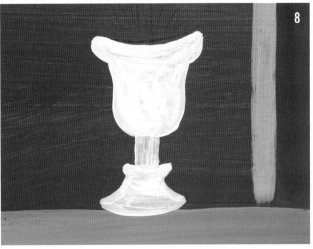

8 BLOCK IN TOPIARY URN

Paint the topiary urns next to the door with White using the no. 4 round. Also paint any other pots hanging against the building walls with White. The terra-cotta pots will not show up against the building color. You can only use terra-cotta pots against the windows.

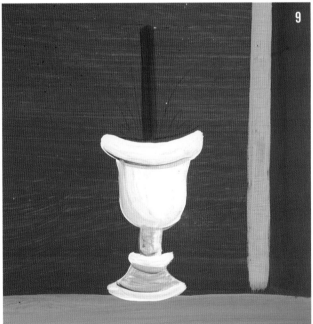

9 DETAIL URN

Use the no. 4 round to shade the urn with Burnt Umber on the lower left sides of each section. With the same brush, add the trunk to the topiary tree with Burnt Umber and Black.

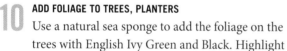

10 **ADD FOLIAGE TO TREES, PLANTERS**
Use a natural sea sponge to add the foliage on the trees with English Ivy Green and Black. Highlight with Old Parchment.

Paint greenery in all of the hanging baskets. Use the no. 4 round to dot in green leaves. The geranium blooms are Barn Red and White. Paint the ferns in the hanging baskets with a no. 0 liner.

11 **PAINT TOPIARY**
Use a scruffy no. 10 flat to paint the topiary with English Ivy Green and Black. Highlight with Old Parchment. I made my topiaries cone shaped, but you can prune them to be any shape you wish (circular, double stacked, etc.). Add sprigs of grass coming out of the urn with a no. 4 round and English Ivy Green, Black and Old Parchment.

12 **BLOCK IN TABLE, CHAIRS**
Basecoat the chairs and table with White and shade with Black to create the gray. Use a no. 8 round.

13

14

15

13 DETAIL TABLE, CHAIRS

Load the no. 4 round with Black and paint the stripes on the chairs and the table base. Use a no. 0 liner to paint the chair arms and legs and the table legs. Paint the coffee cup on the table with Black and White to make a gray.

14 PLACE BICYCLE

Paint the bicycle with the no. 4 round. Start by painting the tires Black. It is tricky to paint the tires in one continuous stroke, so if you're not happy with them, wipe them off with a damp paper towel right away and try again. The seat and handlebars are also Black.

Add the spokes, chain wheel and the rest of the handlebars with the no. 0 liner and Pure Silver plus a touch of White. Add some Black to the bottom of the chain wheel.

15 FINISH BICYCLE

With the no. 4 round and Barn Red, add the rest of the bicycle frame. Paint the pedals and the hubs of the wheels Black. Add White highlights to the wheel hubs, the black part of the handlebars and the seat.

tip Pure Silver is a very transparent color. Adding a touch of White helps make the paint more opaque so you get better coverage.

16

16 ADD CLOTHESLINE

Paint the clothes on the clothesline with the no. 4 round.

Basecoat the dress with Winter Blue. Shade with Deep Midnight Blue and highlight with White.

The socks are White shaded with a bit of Black to make gray along the left side. The stripes are Winter Blue.

The boxers are Old Parchment shaded with Burnt Umber. The hearts are Barn Red.

Use a no. 0 liner and thinned White to paint the clothesline across the two windows. Paint little bows at the ends of the line. Add little clothespins with small strokes of Country Tan.

17

17 ADD FINAL DETAILS

Reinstate any trim lines over the pots and other embellishments in the windows. Add cast shadows around all of the elements with a no. 8 round and thinned Black (see page 13).

The cat in the window is painted with Cocoa. Add highlights with Antique White. The tiger stripes are Burnt Umber. The features and whiskers are Burnt Umber as well.

Indicate bricks on various sections of the piece by using a no. 0 liner and thinned Burnt Umber. Paint rectangular shapes in clusters to give the faint look of bricks.

Use the 2-inch (51mm) chip brush to paint the top with two coats of black.

17

17

THE FINISHED TOWN-HOUSE DRESSER

ABOVE: The front of the finished town-house dresser.

TOP RIGHT: The left side of the finished town-house dresser.

BOTTOM RIGHT: The right side of the finished town-house dresser.

trompe l'oeil french doors

Flat, sliding doors can transform any room if they are painted to look like French doors with a view. I started with just plain white doors and taped off the grid work. Then my brush was free to roam to create a backyard scene with a girl on a tree swing. Watch your mural start to come to life as you remove the tape (a very gratifying step) and learn how to shade the grid work. Everyone will think the French doors are real and will reach for the faux handle. Add some flowerpots and clouds, and you'll always have a sunny day just outside your door!

materials

BRUSHES
½-inch (13mm) and ¾-inch (19mm) flat, No. 10 flat, No. 0 liner, Nos. 4 and 8 rounds

PALETTE
Apple Barrel Acrylics: Black, Country Tan, English Ivy Green, Lavender, White

DecoArt Americana Acrylics: Celery Green, Deep Midnight Blue, Desert Sand, Winter Blue, Yellow Ochre

Delta Ceramcoat Acrylics: Burnt Sienna, Burnt Umber, Medium Flesh, Metallic Gold, Old Parchment

OTHER MATERIALS
1-inch (25mm) painter's tape, 4-foot (1.2m) level, Carbon transfer paper (optional), Cloud Sponge by Plaid, Gray watercolor pencil or graphite pencil, Natural sea sponge, Pink chalk pencil, Scruffy brush, Yardstick or tape measure

PAINTING THE TROMPE L'OEIL DOORS

Paint the surface white. Measure out a rectangle that will be your glass. My mural was 19 inches (48cm) wide by 68¼ inches (1.7m) high from the outside taped edges. Use 1-inch (25mm) painter's tape to mark off the outside edges. Now divide your width so it is three panes wide (or four if your area is wider). Be sure to figure in 1 inch (25mm) between each pane for the window trim. Divide your height so the door is seven panes high. Again, be sure to factor in 1 inch (25mm) between each pane for trim.

tip Once you get all the tape on the grid finished, hit each edge of the tape with your background color (in this case, White) to help seal the tape to the wall and keep the colors from bleeding under. This will save you a lot of time later.

1 BASECOAT SKY

After you have sealed your tape with White (see Tip above), decide how much sky and grass you want in your mural and mark them off. Don't let a trim line be your horizon line. Make the horizon a little ways below or above a grid line so it is visible.

Basecoat the sky Winter Blue with the Cloud Sponge. Paint right over the tape, but don't go outside the outer perimeter. Let dry.

2 DARKEN SKY, PAINT GRASS

Darken the sky at the top by adding Deep Midnight Blue to Winter Blue. As you move closer to the horizon line, add White to the Winter Blue.

Paint the grass with the Cloud Sponge and English Ivy Green. Use horizontal strokes. Again, paint right over the tape. Let dry and then lighten the grass with Celery Green near the horizon. The grass gets darker as it approaches the bottom of the door, so use less Celery Green and leave it straight English Ivy Green.

3 PAINT DISTANT TREE LINE

Use a small natural sea sponge loaded with English Ivy Green and Black to tap on the distant foliage at the horizon line at various heights so it looks like natural growth. Then wipe out the sponge and pick up English Ivy Green and Old Parchment to add the highlights, focusing on the top left sides of the bushes. Paint the evergreen tree in the same way but create more of a cone shape.

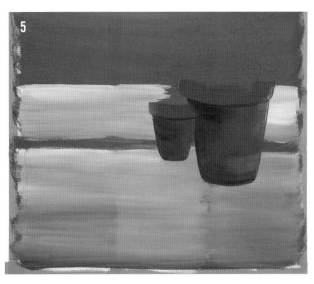

4 BLOCK IN CONCRETE SLAB

For the concrete slab, load the Cloud Sponge with Black and White and block in the area. The gray is lighter at the top of the slab and darker at the bottom so use more White at the top and more Black at the bottom. Let dry.

Now that all of the background is laid in, freehand sketch the design or use carbon paper to transfer the elements onto the surface.

5 BLOCK IN, SHADE FLOWERPOTS

Switch to the ¾-inch (19mm) flat brush and basecoat the flowerpots with Burnt Sienna. Let dry. For shading, load the ¾-inch (19mm) flat with Burnt Sienna and then pick up some Black. The first shading is placed under the collar of the pot. Your stroke should be curved to follow the shape of the pot. The left side is shaded darker than the right side.

6 HIGHLIGHT FLOWERPOTS

For the highlights on the flowerpots, load the ¾-inch (19mm) flat with Burnt Sienna and White. Highlight the entire collar of the pots as well as the right sides. Wipe out the brush and pick up Burnt Sienna to blend the edge of the highlights. Make sure your strokes are curving to follow the shape of the pots, and make sure the pots are curved at the bottoms.

7 FILL IN FLOWERPOTS

Load a natural sea sponge with English Ivy Green and Black and tap in some moss above the pots to fill them in. The back of the greenery should curve so it's not straight across.

125

8 ADD LEAVES

Use a ½-inch (13mm) flat to paint the leaves in the flowerpots. Load the brush with English Ivy Green and Black and basecoat in the basic leave shape (a teardrop shape). While the leaf color is still wet, add a highlight of Old Parchment.

Use the no. 0 liner and Old Parchment mixed with a little bit of English Ivy Green to paint the veins on the leaves.

9 PAINT FLOWERS

Paint the flowers with the no. 8 round and Old Parchment with a touch of Yellow Ochre to make the color darker. For the daisies, start at the outer tip of the petal and pull into the center. Lift up on the pressure as you reach the center. It's kind of a push-and-drag stroke. Add White to the flower color as you paint the top petals.

For some of the flowers, only put petals around the bottom so it looks like you are looking at the flower from the side.

10 DETAIL FLOWERS

The flower centers are Burnt Umber and a touch of White, still using the no. 8 round. Move left to right with an arching brushstroke to create the centers. Then float some Black in at the base of each of the centers. Clean the brush and use White to highlight the centers.

The flowers in the small pot are White. Use the same technique as you did for the other flowers, but make these blooms a little smaller. The centers of these flowers are Yellow Ochre and a touch of White. Float in Burnt Umber to shade the centers and add a White highlight.

Use the no. 4 round and English Ivy Green and Black to place stems for the flowers and leaves. Wherever there is a flower or leaf, just pull a stem into the center of the flowerpot.

11 SHADE AROUND FLOWERPOTS

Use a no. 8 round to float some watery Black around the flowerpots and between them for shadow (see page 13).

12 PAINT TREE TRUNK

Switch to the ½-inch (13mm) flat and pick up Burnt Umber and some Black to basecoat the tree the swing will be attached to. Use two coats for full coverage. Let the paint dry between coats. Also add the trunk of the evergreen using the same colors and brush.

Add vertical highlights to the left side of the tree with White.

tip You can customize and embellish this outdoor scene any way you choose. Here's your chance to add a birdbath, a small pond, pets, even a cat sitting at the door waiting to come in.

13 ADD LEAVES TO TREE

With a damp natural sea sponge, apply leaves to the tree with English Ivy Green and Black. Dab the sponge against the wall to apply the paint. The coverage doesn't need to be solid. You can let some sky show through as it would in nature. Also give the tree an irregular shape and edge so it will look more natural. It shouldn't be symmetrical or a round ball. Lessen the pressure you use to apply the paint as you reach the outer edge of the tree so the edge is softer and blends into the sky.

While the paint is still wet, add Old Parchment for the highlights in select areas where the tops of branches would be. Use the highlights to create contrast and indicate internal shapes within the tree.

14 PAINT SWING

Switch to the no. 10 flat to paint the swing. The ropes are Country Tan. Use the chisel edge of the brush and pull straight down. Keep your hand still and move your entire arm to make this straight line. The seat is Burnt Umber with Country Tan at its bottom. You only need to paint the sides that will be visible as the rest is covered by the girl.

15 BASECOAT GIRL

With the no. 4 round, basecoat the girl on the swing using the following colors: Medium Flesh for the skin, Desert Sand for the hair, Lavender for the dress, White for the hat and socks and Black for the shoes.

16 SHADE, HIGHLIGHT GIRL

Still using the no. 4 round, shade the skin with Burnt Sienna. For the lighter skin tones add White to the Medium Flesh. Add Burnt Umber to Desert Sand to shade the hair. Add White to Desert Sand to highlight the hair. Add Burnt Umber to Lavender to shade the dress and add White to Lavender for the highlights. Add Burnt Umber to White to shade the white areas.

17 RENDER FACIAL FEATURES

Use a no. 0 liner and Burnt Umber to paint the features on the girl's face. Add a tiny Black dot in the middle of each eye. The lips are Burnt Sienna with White for the teeth. The buttons and stitching on the dress are Old Parchment.

To add blush to the checks, rub a dry, scruffy brush over a pink chalk pastel and place the color on the cheeks.

Add any additional shading where you feel it is necessary, such as along the neck, for more contrast.

18 ADD DETAIL GRASS.

Use a no. 4 round to place sprigs of tall grass at the base of the tree. Mix English Ivy Green and Black to place dark grass first. Start at the bottom of the grass and pull up. For lighter grass mix English Ivy Green and Old Parchment and place these blades on top of the dark grass you just painted. Also paint areas of taller grass wherever you would like around the mural.

With a no. 8 round, float Black under the tufts of grass to shade them and help set them into the mural. Place this shadow under the girl as well.

19 ADD CLOUDS

Use a sea sponge and White to paint the clouds (see page 15). Make the clouds heavier at the top and then turn the sponge to the clean edge and work the color down so the clouds don't look too heavy. Make sure your sponge is not too wet.

20 REMOVE TAPE

Once you have completely finished adding elements to the outdoor scene, carefully remove all the grid tape.

21 MARK OFF TRIM LINES

Use a ruler to measure in ¼ inch (6mm) from each edge of the grid, creating a ½ inch (13mm) area in the center of each grid line. Connect these marks with a 4-foot (1.2m) level using a pencil. Put a little diagonal line to connect the corners—like a miter line.

tip It's very helpful to use a water-soluble pencil, such as a gray watercolor pencil, to mark off your trim. The lines will dissolve with water and blend nicely when you apply shading to the trim.

22 SHADE TRIM

Apply shading to the left sides and the bottoms of the grids. Use very thin Black and the no. 10 flat to apply the shading. The paint is so thin it's almost like watercolor. The shading stops at the miter line. It does not go all the way up the grids. Add a darker line at all the miter edges.

Clean your brush well. Wet your brush with clean water and go across the pencil lines on the right and tops of the trim. If you used a water-soluble pencil, the line will soften, and it won't look like you forgot to erase the line. It also will give you just a hint of gray to show the edge of the trim. Wipe out any overlapping ruler lines you don't need.

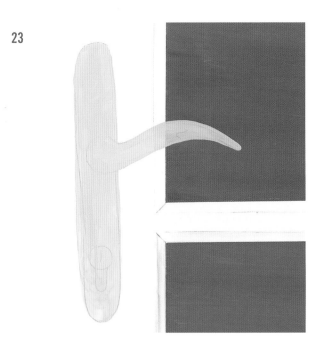

23 BASECOAT DOOR HANDLE

Use the no. 10 flat to basecoat the door handle with Desert Sand.

24 DETAIL DOOR HANDLE

Use the no. 10 flat to paint over the handle with Metallic Gold. The metallic paint is very transparent, so the Desert Sand basecoat helps give the paint full coverage. Shade the handle with Burnt Umber. The shading goes on the left side and on the bottom of the handle. Highlight with White. Don't mix the shading color or the highlight color with the metallic paint. The resulting color will be very muddy. Use a no. 4 round and Burnt Umber to paint the keyhole area.

patterns

The patterns on pages 132–142 may be hand traced or photocopied for personal use only.

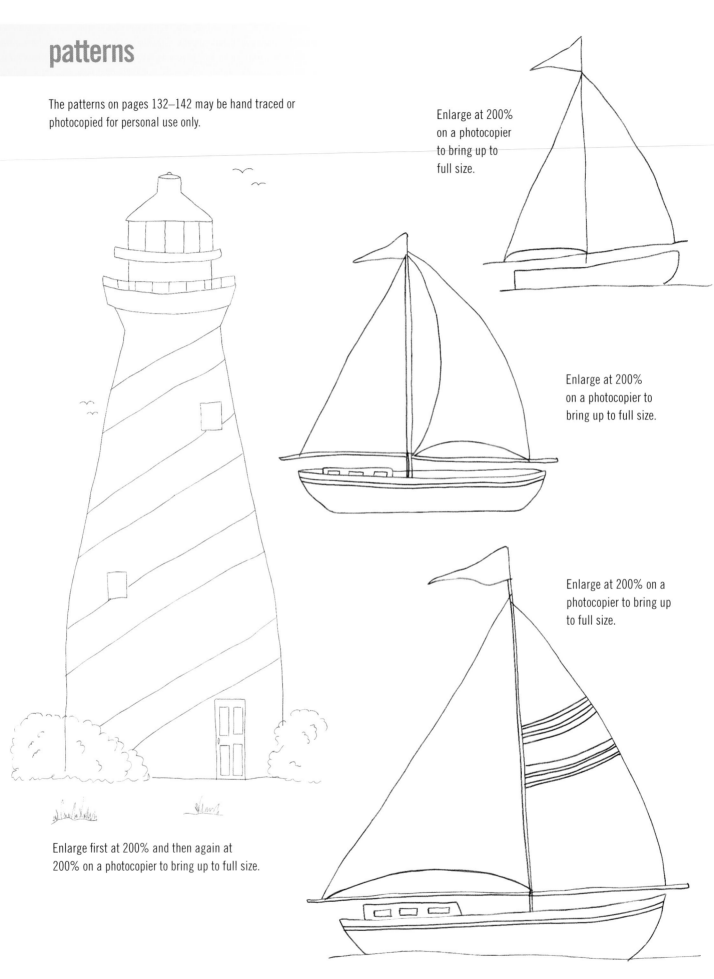

Enlarge at 200% on a photocopier to bring up to full size.

Enlarge at 200% on a photocopier to bring up to full size.

Enlarge at 200% on a photocopier to bring up to full size.

Enlarge first at 200% and then again at 200% on a photocopier to bring up to full size.

Life's a Beach.

Enlarge at 200% and then at 102% on a photocopier to bring up to full size.

Enlarge at 200% on a photocopier to bring up to full size.

Enlarge at 200% on a photocopier to bring up to full size.

Enlarge at 111% on a photocopier to bring up to full size.

Enlarge at 111% on a photocopier to bring up to full size.

Enlarge at 111% on a photocopier to bring up to full size.

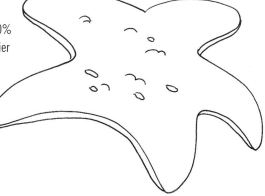

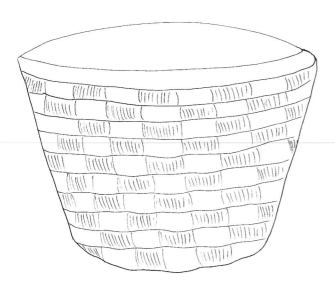

Enlarge at 200% and then at 143% on a photocopier to bring up to full size.

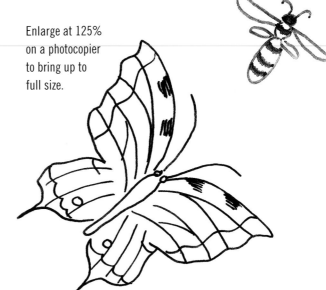

Reproduce at actual size.

Enlarge at 125% on a photocopier to bring up to full size.

Enlarge at 200% and then at 125% on a photocopier to bring up to full size.

Enlarge at 200% on a photocopier to bring up to full size.

Enlarge first at 200% and then again at 200% on a photocopier to bring up to full size.

Enlarge at 172% on a photocopier to bring up to full size.

Enlarge at 200% and then at 119% on a photocopier to bring up to full size.

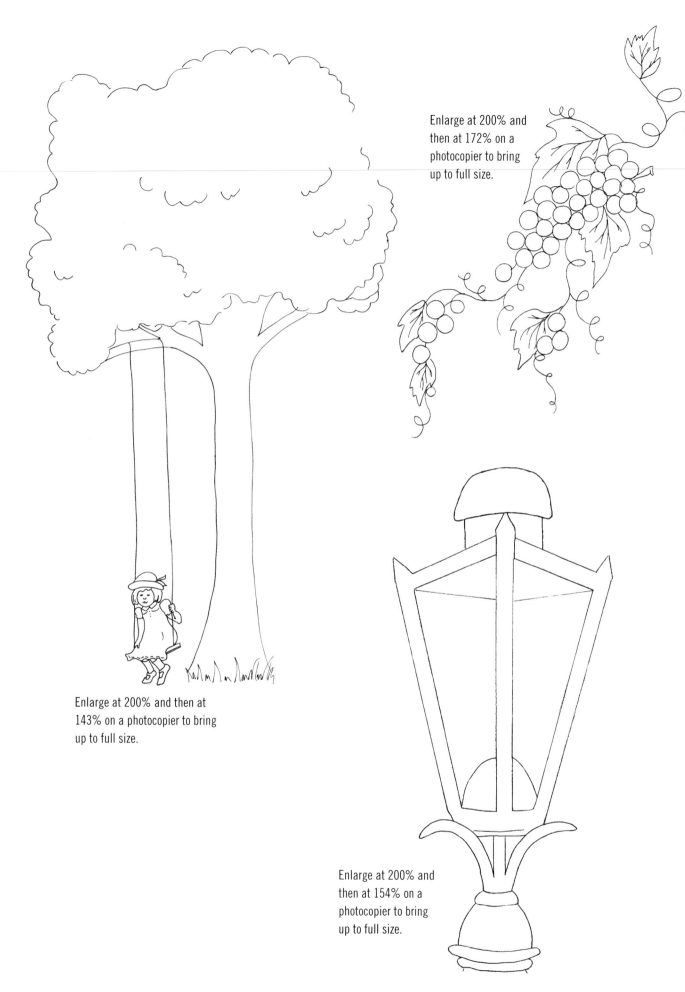

Enlarge at 200% and then at 172% on a photocopier to bring up to full size.

Enlarge at 200% and then at 143% on a photocopier to bring up to full size.

Enlarge at 200% and then at 154% on a photocopier to bring up to full size.

Enlarge at 200% and then at 167% on a photocopier to bring up to full size.

Enlarge at 200% and then at 119% on a photocopier to bring up to full size.

Enlarge first at 200% and then again at 200% on a photocopier to bring up to full size.

Enlarge at 200% and then at 125% on a photocopier to bring up to full size.

Enlarge at 133% on a photocopier to bring up to full size.

Enlarge at 167% on a photocopier to bring up to full size.

Enlarge at 182% on a photocopier to bring up to full size.

Enlarge at 133% on a photocopier to bring up to full size.

Enlarge at 125% on a photocopier to bring up to full size.

Enlarge at 125% on a photocopier to bring up to full size.

Enlarge at 133% on a photocopier to bring up to full size.

Enlarge at 133% on a photocopier to bring up to full size.

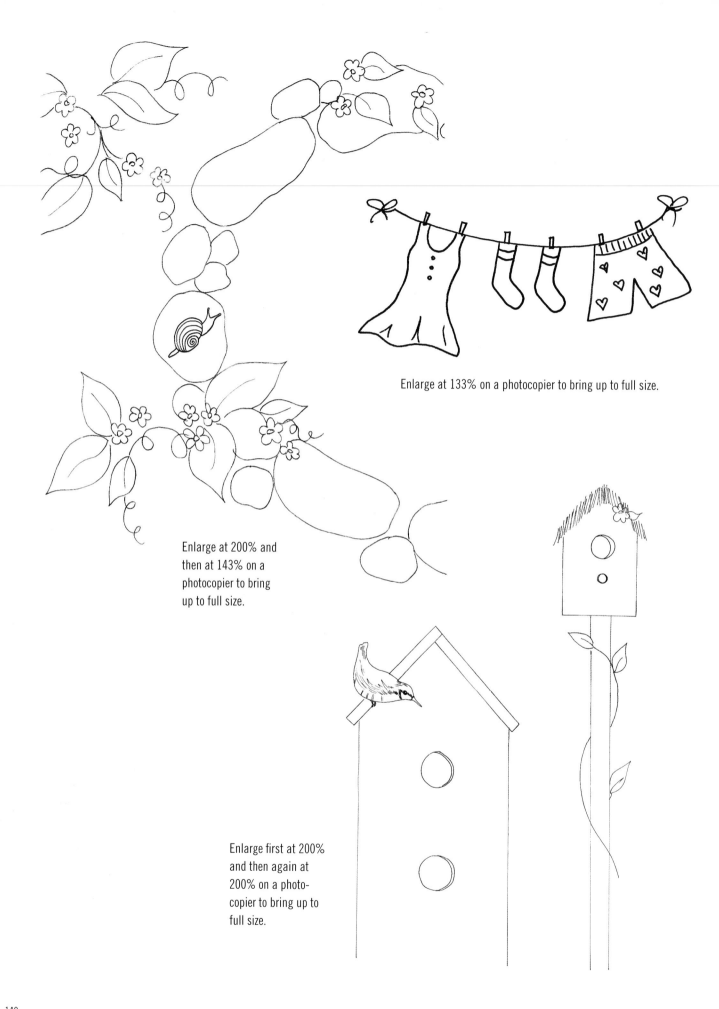

Enlarge at 133% on a photocopier to bring up to full size.

Enlarge at 200% and then at 143% on a photocopier to bring up to full size.

Enlarge first at 200% and then again at 200% on a photo-copier to bring up to full size.

Enlarge at 111% on a photocopier to bring up to full size.

Enlarge at 118% on a photocopier
to bring up to full size.

Enlarge at 182% on a photocopier to bring up to full size.

Enlarge at 128%
on a photocopier to
bring up to full size.

Enlarge at 139% on a photocopier to bring up to full size.

Enlarge at 200% and then at 119% on a photocopier to bring up to full size.

Enlarge at 200% and then at 125% on a photocopier to bring up to full size.

Enlarge at 200% and then at 119% on a photocopier to bring up to full size.

Enlarge at 164% on a photocopier to bring up to full size.

the best in **mural painting** **instruction** is from NORTH LIGHT BOOKS

MURAL PAINTING SECRETS FOR SUCCESS

Internationally known muralist and faux finisher Gary Lord shares his secrets for painting fantastic murals following the latest trends, including holographic metallics, 3-D effect paints and stained concrete. In addition to the twenty-three step-by-step demonstrations, a gallery of more than twenty inspirational photos provides great ideas for you and your clients. Follow Gary and other professional mural painters' expert advice on running a successful mural painting business, including how to network and market, negotiate contracts and price and work effectively. From black-light planets to classical realism, this book shows you the way and the means to create what your client wants!

ISBN-13: 978-1-58180-980-0; ISBN-10: 1-58180-980-8; PAPERBACK, 160 PAGES, #Z0816

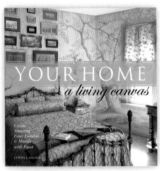

YOUR HOME: A LIVING CANVAS

Adding décor elements can give your home new life. This treasure trove of inspiration is filled with examples of added effects as well as stunning photography of finished rooms. Author and artist Curtis Heuser guides you room by room through his renovated Victorian home. Along the way you'll learn how to create unique paint effects, pick up tips on everything from colors to contractors and be swept up to new inspirational levels.

ISBN-13: 978-1-58180-783-7; ISBN-10: 1-58180-783-X; HARDCOVER, 144 PAGES, #33453

CREATIVE KIDS' MURALS YOU CAN PAINT

More than fifty whimsical wall paintings offer you a range of unique ideas, themes and color combinations, complete with thirty-two step-by-step demonstrations that make these murals easy and fun to re-create on your own walls. The fun and whimsical mural designs are adaptable for any child's room—everything from nursery and magical themes to animals, flowers and sports.

ISBN-13: 978-1-58180-805-6; ISBN-10: 1-58180-805-4; PAPERBACK, 128 PAGES, #33484

DECORATIVE FURNITURE WITH DONNA DEWBERRY

In this inspiring guide, Donna Dewberry demonstrates her trademark one-stroke painting technique in ten all-new projects designed especially for furniture. You learn how to achieve a realistic look in your murals—from soft florals and meandering vines to ripe cherries and delicate china painted on dressers, desks, tables and folding screens.

ISBN-13: 978-1-58180-016-6; ISBN-10: 1-58180-016-9; PAPERBACK, 128 PAGES, #31662

These books and other fine North Light titles are available at your local arts and crafts retailers bookstore or from online suppliers. Please visit our Web site at www.artistsnetwork.com.

3 6058 00162 9555